Life in the Lancashire Milltowns

For REX & HANNAH BRINDLE
formerly of Blackburn

Life in the Lancashire Milltowns

by

W R Mitchell

Foreword by Thelma Barlow
of "Coronation Street"

CASTLEBERG
1997

He was the sort of man who couldn't blow his nose without lamenting the demise of the Lancashire cotton industry.

Cyril Connolly, referring to George Orwell.

Take Lancashire and all it stands for from Britain and at once we become an unimportant storm-bound island lost in the mists of the north.

Walter Greenwood (1951).

They don't waste time in Lancashire... "Owt?" says the salesman. "Nowt," says the buyer. Then, if they are friends, they may discuss the cricket scores, and Yorkshire's chances against Lancashire; if not, the salesman goes and there's an end of it, until he calls again.

Harold Brighouse and Charles Forrest, in the novel of Hobson's Choice (1917).

A **Castleberg** Book.

First published in the United Kingdom in 1997.

ISBN 1 871064 78 3

Typeset in Palacio, printed and bound in the United Kingdom by Lamberts Printers, Station Road, Settle, North Yorkshire, BD24 9AA.

Published by Castleberg, 18 Yealand Avenue, Giggleswick, Settle, North Yorkshire, BD24 0AY.

Contents

Foreword by Thelma Barlow
Seasonal recollections by Mike Harding

Cover design: John Thomlinson
Drawings by Christine Denmead and Ruth Blackburn

Foreword

by
Thelma Barlow
(of Granada Television's *Coronation Street*)

YOU might consider it odd that a Yorkshirewoman should be writing an introduction to a book about Lancashire, but I claim the right by dint of association, having spent the last twenty-five years of my life working in *Coronation Street.*

I first met Bill Mitchell when I moved back into my home county and he came to interview me about my Yorkshire past and my Lancashire present. I soon realised that here was a modest man whose knowledge of the area is awesome and this he can impart in his books with a great warmth and affection for the people and places about which he writes.

The past 150 years have seen a remarkable change in the way of life of the people of Lancashire, and in this book it's our good fortune to have a chronicler who will give us a flavour of the area as true and typical as a dish of Lancashire hot pot or tripe and onions.

Always in the midst of meticulously researched facts there is an enthusiasm which is enriched with curious or amusing anecdotes—this is Bill Mitchell's style—and nowhere more evident and effective than when taking us on a journey through *Life in the Lancashire Milltowns.*

The Knocker-up.
Sleepy voices called back "aa reet."

Introduction

WAS IT truly the world's first industrial revolution, based on textiles, which transformed the appearance and social life of Lancashire so that by the end of the nineteeth century about one-third of the county was covered by mills, terraced houses, flagstones and cobbles? Indeed it was.

Milltowns were mucky. Natural beauty wilted as industrial areas were grafted on to historic places. Villages half as old as time began to sprawl as new factories and terraced housing were tastelessly interminged, bound together by tram lines and a patina of soot. Milltowns were not just for Lancastrians. People from all parts of the land arrived, eager for work. They included Irish folk, whose immediate ancestors suffered the trauma of the Great Hunger. Here, too, and especially in the string of newly enlarged towns in East Lancashire, were folk from the northern dales of Yorkshire, where lead-mining had collapsed in the face of cheap imports from Spain.

King Cotton used handy natural resources—stone wrenched from the moorsides, a copious supply of soft water from the gritstone hills, and locally-mined coal to keep the fires in the mill boilers cherry-red. Even the grey skies and damp air were suited to textile production. If the air dried, and the yarn was affected, the mill-owner turned on steam pipes to regulate the humidity. Harold Brighouse, in Hobson's Choice, in the novel of his play about Milltown life and characters, wrote of "cotton-mill operatives, stunted by generations of labour in moist and heated air."

Lancashire had its heyday. Then the momentum was lost, for a variety of reasons, some of them economic and others political. The losers were the grey mass of the people. Yet though sixty per cent of the cotton material used in Britain today is imported, Lancashire weaves on. The nose-cone of an advanced aircraft, Concorde, was woven at Colne on a fifty-year-old Lancashire loom, but the looms in use today are high tech. and automatic, achieving levels of production undreamed of in th'owd days, when hundreds of little looms chattered to themselves in a shed with overhead shafting and draughts created by miles of leather belting.

There is pride in the past, when King Cotton had his palace in Manchester and used Liverpool as a seaport to import raw material; when Lancashire mills met the home needs for cotton fabric before breakfast and exported the rest of the day's production, mainly to the Empire which occupied three-quarters of the world. My concern when writing *Life in the Lancashire Milltowns* was to record folk tales of the immediate past—the recollections of those who remember when a forest of blackened chimneys belched smoke and ash, creating a fug which cleared one week in fifty-two. Then those who'd managed to save a bit o' brass had a lemming-like dash to the seaside at Blackpool.

All the old folk I met recalled the tattoo of clog-irons against flagstones as the workers commuted, a human tide, flowing and ebbing to the commands of mill buzzers. A latecomer was fined—or locked out. At one mill, the boss said to a laggard: ''Buzzers gone.'' The worker replied: ''They'll pinch owt these days.''

The profitability of Lancashire cotton depended largely on a 'reservoir' of cheap labour, with children joining the weaving mills as half-timers, unpaid until they were trained, when for a while they received no more than five shillings a week. If working conditions had been better, they would still have been dreadful.

A woman in a weaving shed, clad in blouse and long skirt over which was spread a 'warkin' brat' or apron, stood in her clogs on the stone flags and, with chattering teeth, applied herself to a monotonous job for many hours at a time. There was no direct sunlight. The saw-toothed roof lights—Lancashire's Northern Lights—kept out the direct rays of the sun so there would be enough moisture to keep the yarn happy. Nowt else mattered.

For a dynamic century, Milldom grew, throve, wobbled and went into dramatic decline. A few bosses did very well, thank you, during the boom years and when the government paid them for closing down mills. Bosses lived on at stately homes on the hills, away from Milltown muck, or they retired to Windermere or St Annes.

The host of working folk were enslaved by economic necessity. For them, there was little else but bed and work. The Lancashire 'lass' of song and story, who remained chirpy despite enormous difficulties, was personified by Gracie Fields, of Rochdale. Our Gracie cheered us up with such songs as *Sing as We Go* and, sentimentally, *Sally*, the pride of our alley. (An alley was the space between two rows of looms). Gracie, who started work in a spinning mill, eventually did better than the average Lancashire lass about whom she sang.

The real-life Lancashire lass, who was anyone between fourteen and death, was paid for what she produced. If she was ill or late to work, there was no butter on the bread at home. Her face was pale and drawn, her body scarred by shuttles which had leapt from looms like missiles, and her shoulders were bent from working long hours at the mill, fetching weft and carrying finished cloth. When Sally was not scrattin' at th'mill, she had a home to keep, often with a drunken husband to humour. She reared a big family, washed, iron and baked and went to bed with her spine creaking under the strain.

I have known some of the Lancashire Milltowns since childhood. My grandfather, a Dorset man, was one of a host of people sucked into Lancashire textiles at a time when 'brass' was scarce and life was cheap. My father, born in a Lancashire Milltown, recalled without pleasure or humour, when the family had to make a midnight flit, willing but unable to pay the landlord his dues. He also remembered when Margaret Bonfield, one of the Labour pioneers, came to tea. Uncle Henry and his family lived at Burnley, and so over many years I kept in touch with the land west of the Pennines.

I heard some fascinating tales, such as the origin of one of the rumours which swept the country in the 1914-18 war. When a troop train from Scotland drew in to a Burnley platform, a porter asked one of the soldiers where he came from. The reply was "Ross-shire". The porter, being unable to understand much of what the soldiers were saying, thought he said "Russia". The story which alarmed the country was that Russian troops had landed and (an imaginative touch) they had snow on their boots!

As the dawn of a new millenium approaches, urban Lancashire looks at the world with a gleaming face and a diversity of industries. Conditions have changed dramatically since the day when Leary Constantine was the only dark-faced man at Nelson. He was a folk hero because of his prowess on the cricket field. Later he had a successful career in politics in his native West Indies. Today, rather more than half of the textile operatives are of Asian origin. Many of the places of worship are domed.

The Lancashire knack of absorbing strangers and making them feel at home continues to the present day.

A General View

THE COAL MAN

LANCASHIRE Milltowns were distinctive, separated from their neighbours by a few fields, even cornfields. Little farms at the edges of the towns provided the milk and dairy products needed by a large urban populace. A Milltown courting couple could go for a walk in the country. Some towns in East Lancashire had attractive situations. Terraced housing framed distant views of wooded cloughs leading the eyes up to hilltops fringed with heather. Old Pendle crowned the skyline.

Today, what used to be Milltowns are strung together by motorways, by bungaloid development and by miles of sodium chloride street lighting which glows orange and stains the underbellies of passing clouds. What used to be vacant, wine-red moorland now sprouts television transmitter aerials or even 'wind farms'. The prevailing wind blows clean and cool. Sheep which on the moors to the east of town were a few shades darker in grey because of the polluted air now have their natural colour. With clean-air legislation, it is not easy to recall when Milldom had a forest of chimneys which breathed black smoke into the air and, with a change of wind direction, send it coursing along the streets themselves. Even the sparrows had a dry cough.

Not only mill chimneys broke the skyline. Here, too, were the steeples of churches built in the Gothic style, as opposed to the much plainer Nonconformist chapels, though both would come from the same quarry—that dark scar on the hillside, a mile or so away. The mill-owners needed a large and handy labour force. Into being came a gridiron of terrace housing. Walter Greenwood, author of *Love on the Dole,* wrote about Salford that "a street led into another street and into another until the brain reeled, stunned in a maze of sameness." In the semi-rural districts, as W T Arnold noted, was "the frayed edge of urban Lancashire, where the factory hooter wakes the grouse, and you hear the clogs, before dawn, tapping a dotted line of sound through peat and bracken."

Darkness lay across the face of the earth. Except in late summer, when for a week or two the bonnie heather bloomed, the moors had a range of dark tones—the mid-brown of millstone grit, evident in an outcrop or a dry-stone wall; the peat as dark and moist as chocolate cake, and all thatched with coarse grasses and the stiff heather stalks. The general dullness was relieved by reservoirs, mirrors which reflected the sky, usually grey but at times blue, with a few cumulus cloud, like galleons under full sail, across the azure spaces.

Near Manchester, the builders used trillions of red bricks. Multi-storied spinning mills blushed in the hard evening sunlight. Terraces of brick looked positively cheerful as the days lengthened in spring' when dandelions appeared from cracks in the pavement and rhubarb in the allotment opened its sappy umbrella to the April showers.

The Milltowns, bonded to each each other by metal rails, on which trams operated, were by no means all red brick. To the north-east, near the gritstone hills, dressed stone was used for building. Between Burnley and Colne, both the type and quality of the housing was an improvement on those nearer Manchester. In East Lancashire, moorland provided a backdrop to almost every view. Moorland was loved and feared. A garage sign proclaimed: "Fill up for the Moors", as though a motorist's life depended on having a full tank. Yet only half a dozen miles lay between the home valley and its Yorkshire neighbour.

The 'lungs' of a Milltown was the park, given, named after and holding the statue of the industrialist who had donated it to the greater glory of the town and of himself. On Sunday afternoon, you could hardly move in the cemetery without colliding with family parties wearing their best clothes. They were not just out for a walk. Every gravestone inscription prompted gossip between friends of the dear-departed. Many a Milltown lad proposed to his lady-love near the family grave.

Back home, the indomitable Milltown housewife continued to fight a war on two fronts—poverty and pollution. It was calculated that seven tons of soot fell on each square mile of Bolton per annum. When industrial pollution was being discussed at Blackburn, someone mentioned the concept of smokeless zones. The secretary of the weavers' union, concerned about the shortage of work, said: "I wish I could see more smoke coming out of our mill chimneys."

The main smell of the old Milltown was compounded of hot engine oil and textiles. The rhythmic clatter of machinery on every hand testified to Victorian and Edwardian mill-owners and workers alike that all was well with the world.

Life on Nob Hill

On the hillside at the west side of town, where the breezes came fresh from the Irish Sea, could be found the homes of the 'nobs'—mill-owners, solicitors, bankers and the like. They were at the peak of the Milltown social pyramid—a pyramid which was supported by the grey mass of the people. The 'nobs' could sing with gusto the hymn *All Things Bright and Beautiful* because, for them, it was. And most of them were not embarrassed by the verse (since deleted) which implied that God had ordered the status of rich and poor.

It is dangerous to generalise. The old families who benefited from industrialisation lived in their big houses by the right of many generations. The new-rich included those who were 'all show' and 'hadn't a penny to scratch their bottom with'. When a Lancashire millowner employed Lutyens, the best-known architect, to design him a new house, he was not to know that ere long the Slump would occur. People thought of him as mean when, indeed, his financial reserves were dangerously low.

Some mill-owners lived in villages and continued to live in the ancestral big house close to their factories. They bought themselves seats in heaven by generous donations towards the local church or chapel. Yet one of the four-loom weavers considered herself lucky when, as she told her family: "I got two papers this week—a pound and a ten shilling note." With some worthy exceptions, Lancashire mill-owners had little regard for the workers. A Blackburn man who rang up the mill to have a brief word with the weaver to whom he was engaged was told: "We don't have weavers in the office." There was little regard for the fledgling unions which sought to improve working conditions.

The owners of weaving sheds who, by day, wandered about in old clothes and knew their workforce by their Christian names went off to their hillside homes and lived a radically different life. Well-established families did not flaunt their weath. The new-rich had ambitions which ranged from being elected t'Mayor to joining the local hunt. Classically, a family with aspirations discovered that "fra clogs to clogs is three generations". The man who established a textile enterprise made it thrive by hard work, economy and shrewd dealing. His son, expensively educated, was more socially inclined and grandson, having little interest in the business and developing social pretensions beyond his class, frittered t'brass away.

The mini-mansions at the edge of town were usually of broad-faced Georgian style and situated behind tall walls and groves of laurel and rhododendrons. Broad steps led to the front door. There was tiling in the hall. It was a house packed with good furniture, potted ferns and numerous ornaments, which were regularly dusted by one of the maids. A house near Blackburn is recalled for the beauty of the candelabra in the dining room and the presence in the big lounge of an expensive pianola.

Employers in the spinning areas, such as Oldham or Rochdale, have been represented in the classic plays about Lancashire mill life. Here were tough businessmen. They'd made 'brass' and they did not intend to squander it on finery. The had few social pretensions and made no special effort to improve their cultural level, their behaviour, manners or attitude to life. Sir Ben Dobson, maker of textile machines, was one of the more gentlemanly type to be found in the Bolton area. He was fascinated by literature and science. He was as much interested in evolutionary creation as making a profit.

Accrington was dominated by the huge mill of the Bullough family, who exported many of the machines which eventually were to undercut the work of the older models left in Lancashire. One of the Bulloughs bought the Hebridean island of Rhum. His son, Sir George, spent over a million pounds at the turn of the century, having a castle built from imported stone and a garden from imported soil. Many other improvements were made to Rhum, though he did not spend more than a few weeks there each year. He was fond of voyaging to distant parts in his private yacht.

The weaving boss was usually a man who had been a weaver and had made good. B Bowker, looking back to the opulent years from 1900 to 1914, told of a weaver who married the daughter of a manufacturer, sold yarn at a half per cent commission on the Manchester Cotton Exchange, became an independent yarn agent and moved to a fine house at Southport. By 1920, he had £150,000 and had bought a yet bigger house at St Annes.

Amos Nelson started work as a half-timer and became a man of such wealth through textiles that (as related) he could use the services of Sir Edwin Lutyens, a celebrated and expensive architect, whom whom he met on a voyage to India. The new Gledstone Hall, near West Marton, followed the theme of Lutyens, which was the old English barn, with capacious roof, and among its features was a grand staircase with alternating white and black marble steps.

A Blackburn electrician who did re-wiring work at a hall, home of a wealthy cotton manufacturer at the edge of Blackburn, was told not to use the main doors and therefore had to carry all the equipment up three-storeys by ladder and enter the place by the attic windows. The family thus continued to live their good life without too much mess. ''They had two maids and a chauffeur for two Buick cars. One of them was used to drive the family of three to St Annes for afternoon tea. There were no cups of tea for the workers.''

In the late 1920s, the owner of a small firm in Colne throve on commission work. His residence was a big house on the edge of town, yet he walked to work, making a point of arriving before 7 a.m., when the door of the mill was locked. Any weaver who was late for work had to stand outdoors until it was re-opened half an hour later. This man appeared to despise his workers. One of his oldest weavers complained of poor-quality yarn and said that before she wove any more she would "gie ower first." The mill-owner told her: "Tha wean't. Tha can't afford." She was, indeed, the only wage-earner in her family. Her father had left home. Mother was ill.

In contrast is the story of a Blackburn mill which employed each generation of some local families. A mother took her daughter to the mill to ask the owner if there was a job for her. He nodded and, putting his arm round the mother, said: "If tha'rt awf as good at weyvin' as thi mother's bin, tha'll do."

Churches and Chapels

The Milltowns had religions suited to every taste and temperament. A Blackburn man who, sixty-five years ago, went on a round of some of them, first attended a large Anglican church. "It was Mayor's Sunday. The Town Clerk was there wearing his wig. The Mayor was in his robes. There was a line up of soldiers, complete with guns. The hymns were not so much being sung as mimed. It was so much out of touch with what I felt about religion, it wasn't my scene at all."

His next call, one day after he had finished work, was at the market square, where orators were trying to whip up the fervour of the crowd. "There was a man with a big moustache—it seemed to extend a foot beyond each side of his face. This was Pastor Jefferies, a man who used to tell people to throw their crutches away. I was fascinated by him. He said to the crowd: 'Do you believe that Jesus Christ is the Son of God and the Saviour of the World?' I put my hand up. The next moment I was swept off my feet and literally carried up the wooden steps to a seat at the front of the platform. The assembled people clapped their hands and jumped about. It was certainly not my scene."

By now, the seeker after a religious experience was, to quote his words, "getting a bit flummoxed." One wet night, at the 'back-end' of the year, he came across Queen's Hall Methodist Mission. "I went into the gallery. Everybody was talking. It was not the atmosphere of a cathedral by any means. Then the minister and his wife came out and the deaconnesses and went on this rostrum. Immediately, there was a hush. And a profound respect. And this man used his lovely baritone voice to sing *Nearer my God to Thee* in the Paul Robeson version and I was deeply moved. The thing which moved we most was the notices. It was practical Christianity. There were to be concerts for the unemployed and an outing for poor children."

In his case, Methodism satisfied his aspirations. He recalls that the minister toured local wholesale butchers and fruiterers and had meat and vegetables given to him. These were cooked in a big boiler in the chapel kitchen. "Then he used to put a muffler on and a cap and go round the streets giving pennies out so that whoever received them might go to the chapel schoolroom for some soup."

In the old Lancashire communities, Anglicanism held sway and ministered to the people. When the Milltowns evolved at a rapid pace, and an influx of people filled houses in the mean streets, it tended to be Nonconformity, with its wide and varied range of chapels, which reached out to the poor and needy. Walter Greenwood was to recall an Established Church when rents were charged for pews. The nameplates of notable people were to be seen engraved in copper at the ends of pews. He added: "Whether it was the snobbery that alienated the ordinary man from the habit of church-going, whether it was the cynicism consequent on two world wars with a terrible slump as the sandwich filling, I do not know."

If a chapel had been built by a mill-owner, he'd order summat big, to impress his fellow citizens. Otherwise, there were run-of-the-mill chapels with striking names—Ebenezer, Jerusalem, Paradise, Salem, Zion, etc. Baptists and Congregationalists predated the Methodists. One of the smaller sects, the Sandemanians, managed to keep a firm foothold on the religious scene. If you were a Methodist, you might have to explain what sort—Wesleyan or Prim. The taciturn folk joined the Quakers.

Milltowns swarmed with Nonconformists, who were generally noted for lusty hymn-singing, thoughtful (long) sermons and, their opposition to 'strong drink'. At Blackburn, Mrs Lewis had her Teetotal Mission which intercepted wage-earners as they went home on Friday evening and tried to persuade them to take the money home rather than spend it at the various pubs. The premises were decorated with classic texts, such as "Lips that touch liquor shall never touch mine." The hymns were slanted towards sobriety. *Cwm Rhonda* was sung to the words: "Save the drunkard, save the drunkard, save him now and ever more." Generally, the theology of the popular hymns was not very good but "they had good tunes—and we liked to bawl our heads off!"

A popular hymn in East Lancashire was *Rimington,* named after a village lying near Pendle Hill. Its composer, Francis Duckworth, was of a family which had moved to Colne, where he became a successful grocer. He was also organist at the Albert Road chapel. His famous tune was published in 1904 and sung for the first time at the Colne Whitsunside processions to the words *Jesus shall Reign where'er the Sun.* The hymn became a special favourite with brass bandsmen and vocal groups, who proliferated in the old Milltowns.

Whitsuntide, a high point in the Church year, saw vast numbers of Sunday School children processing behind banners and bands, the demonstration culminating with hymn singing. Walter Bennett, a Lancashire historian, recorded that at Nelson, one of the smaller towns, in 1901, nine Sunday Schools had a total of 4,500 scholars. Support for Sunday Schools gradually declined and with it the Whit Walks and yet by 1931 a total of 21 schools yielded the quite impressive roll-call of 3,400 scholars.

A chapel pulpit was huge, like the bridge of a coasting vessel, and hollow. A door lead from the back into what was generally known as t'Glory Hole , a receptacle for broken chairs, unwanted books—and the dust of ages. The pipes of the electric organ, situated on the balcony immediately behind the pulpit, almost tickled the ceiling. With a rear-view mirror, the organist could scan the pulpit when, on a musical occasion, it was occupied by a conductor. The pitch-pine pews, each row with its umbrella stand at the end, were varnished and extremely hard. Bum-numbing, indeed.

The choir pews usually overlooked the pulpit. Rows of choristers could follow the course of the sermon by noting the frequency with which the preacher turned over his pages of notes. Faces lightened perceptibly when he got to the last page. If a sermon was being recycled, the preacher was said to be "trotting an old pony out." Sometimes he had fallen back on an old favourite and "his notes are as black as t'fireback."

Oh, those sermons! Sometimes, the preacher was lively and relatively brief. A twenty-minute sermon seemed to be over in a trice. There were verbal fireworks, with much thumping of the Bible to emphasise the key points. The sermon followed the classic formula—introduction, three points, finale. Often the sermon degenerated into a verbal torrent—excited, cliché-ridden. A preacher's occupation was usually reflected in his style of sermonising. An auctioneer preached as though he was trying to sell a wardrobe to an unwilling customer. A grocer's favourite text was from Isaiah, about the darkness which covered the earth. He asked his hearers to imagine 144 times that darkness, which was the gross darkness that covered the people. On summer afternoons, a congregation fought against going to sleep and even God must have nodded.

Thankfully, chapels had a social side. On week-nights, in winter, in addition to prayer meetings and other religious functions, there were special do's such as concerts with a Jacob's Join meal built into the procedure, each person contributing to it. One man was reported to say: "I've more faith than t'lot o' you. I've browt nowt."

Milltown Artists

A Salford artist who became famous for his Milltown studies was L S Lowry. His studies of 'matchstick men' against millscapes were to be transformed into a ballet. Photographers were fond of portraying Lowry in a dingy Milltown setting of lofty chimneys, multi-storied spinning mills and spindly-legged railway viaducts. Lowry, rent collector and cashier-cum-artist, was at home here, with a natural gravity of expression which did not permit him to smile. Well, not often. And the people occupying his red-brick world were a solemn lot.

Lowry was tall, stiffly-built, an intermittent wearer of spectacles and trilby hat. His face was long and lean, the head thatched with hair which was periodically cut—one might almost say 'mown'—in the classic economic style of 'short back and sides'. A natty dresser, complete with jacket and tie, he was none the less so absorbed in his art his clothes were usually spattered with paint.

Lowry lived for eighty-eight years, but few people really knew him. He was a very private person. As a rent-collector, at a time of considerable unemployment and privation, he did at least have a regular and reasonably well paid job. This artist did not starve in an attic, though he liked to think he had suffered privation. Year after year, in the 1920s, a time of industrial depression when thousands of Milltowers grew pale and weak, he bestrode the terraces of Salford coaxing money from tenants. In his old age, when his paintings were selling briskly and he had far more 'brass' than he knew what to do with, he spent much of it on Rosetti paintings, which he kept under the bed for safety.

In his time as a rent-collector, Lowry stored up mental images of his sooty environment and pale-faced inhabitants. He attended art classes for years but it was not until he was sixty that his special talent was recognised by Bernard Taylor, the art reviewer of *The Manchester Guardian* who wrote of his ''interesting and original outlook. . . He emphasises violently everything that industrialism has done to make the aspect of Lancashire more forbidding than that of most other places. . . His Lancashire is grey, with vast rectangular mills towering over diminutive houses. . . If there is an open space, it is of trodden earth. . . The crowds which have this landscape for their background are entirely in keeping with their setting. . .''

It was Taylor who, when he was shown a new Lowry study of Milldom which was very dark, held it up against a dark wall and advised him to paint pictures—even pictures with industrial settings—that would be in greater contrast. Lowry, initially annoyed, was quick to see the sense of this and henceforth he painted almost all his industrial landscapes against a white background.

This artist was very quotable. He said: ''I've a one-track

mind. I only deal with poverty. Always with gloom... You never see the sun in my work. That's because I can't paint shadows." Though ridiculed by the Manchester art establishment, he lived long enough to become a celebrity. The Press loved such an eccentric. *The Times* art critic described the characteristic Lowry man as "clumsy, bulbous boots, spindly legs, short coat with widish skirts, little stick, bowler hat (or cap) jammed well down to his ears."

Lowry was elected as an Associate of the Royal Academy in 1955. The Post Office gave him added renown by issuing a Lowry postage stamp in 1967. His spartan way of life extended into his wealthy old age. He died on February 23, 1976, leaving us a vivid insight into the Lancashire of his youth—a Lancashire which was already in the course of rapid change. He left a host of pictures and some memorable quotations, of which my favourite is: "There's no accounting for tastes. Specially mine."

If Lowry didn't often look happy, Helen Bradley—small, dumpy—invariably had a smile on her face which was transmitted to her work. When I first met Helen Bradley, in 1983, she was in the midst of a wildly creative period, ransacking the lockers of her mind for memories of a childhood in Oldham before the 1914-18 war.

Helen was born in 1900. Sixty years later, residing with her husband Tom, a textile designer, in a small cottage at Cartmel, and having raised two children, she burst on to the art scene with her distinctive Milltown studies. Helen had little formal education because her father thought she would be better off being taught at home. Helen, having had some tuition in art at Oldham, was offered a scholarship with further study in France, but father was 'agin it'.

When quite old, Helen Bradley astonished us by an evocation of Lancashire in the mills-and-muck era. She told me the urge to do this began after she had attended an exhibition of modern art. She felt she could do as well, if not better, than the artists whose work was on view. She met the famous

Lowry, relating incidents from her childhood at Lees, near Oldham, and recalling local characters, especially the prim Miss Carter, who always wore pink. Lowry urged her to include some of these characters in her pictures.

She did, prolifically. Several hundred studies, of various sizes, were painted. Helen's people were much more colourful and relaxed than Lowry's matchstick army. She introduced a touch of Eastern promise, having been influenced by the art of India and the Moghuls. When no brushes were to hand, she used her fingers. On beginning a new work, she fingered on the paint and rubbed it hard into the canvas, creating delicately-tinted areas and misty effects.

Against these, she related stories of childhood as though they were being mimed. Miss Carter appeared on many of the pictures and gave the first of several published collections of her work its title—*Miss Carter Wore Pink.* At Cartmel, those long years ago, Helen showed me a large painting of Blackpool as it was during Oldham Wakes. She had spent a month of almost ceaseless work upon it, for the host of personalities were not based on a stylished figure, endlessly repeated, but individuals, occupying the wide expanses of promenade and sands.

The Wakes were in late September. It was then that Oldham folk moved to the coast for a last fling before the onset of winter. Helen's photographic memory had enabled her to visualise even the weather conditions, with the autumn sun lingering near the horizon. It was the last time in the season the Punch and Judy man was operating.

Helen planned to give some Lancashire paintings themes from the Bible. The Flood would be represented by a tidal wave sweeping through a street of terraced houses, washing her now familiar characters—even the prim Miss Carter—along with it. The last painting to be available as a signed limited edition was not a millscape but a serene study of water and trees with a setting sun, mist and a solitary waterbird. She wrote of her feelings when painting this picture:

"The air is heavy with floating mists, and the waters in the pool are still. Light, go gently into the silent night." She was quoting from an early Chinese poem. Helen Bradley's work undoubtedly had that little touch of Eastern promise...

Our Gracie

If anyone typified the Lancashire mill girl it was Gracie Fields, the Rochdale lass born above a Rochdale chip shop who became world famous as an entertainer, was made a Dame Commander of the British Empire and eventually had a home (and grave) on the Isle of Capri, under a blue Mediterranean sky. Our Gracie was, as far as Milltowners were concerned, and the folk of Rochdale in particular, "the uncrowned queen."

In her autobiography, *Sing as We Go,* she mentioned that when she was born in 1898, her nineteen-year-old mother did not get much encouragement from anyone. "If I were thee," said one long-suffering neignbour above her squawls, "I'd smother yon child in my shawl. Happen we'd all get some sleep then." The voice became silvern.

She was to recall the quietness of the town when the mills were working.The only people stirring in the streets were young children, old folks, with a few mothers carrying babies inside their thick black shawls. On a woman's head, under the shawl, were hair-curlers, "big as mouse-traps." Front doors were rarely latched. A sick woman found that someone had scrubbed her doorstep, washed her pots and put a stew on to simmer without a word. If the identity of the benefactress became known, she would try to make the thanks sound like an insult by saying: "Eeh—that old shin-beef stew? It was either give it thee or give it t'cat."

Who of the older end will forget the image of Gracie in the film *Sing as We Go,* from a script by J B Priestley? It was first screened in the 1930s and cheered us up as we saw her leading a host of millfolk. As far as her native Rochdale is concerned, the figure 8 is important. Gracie arrived screamingly in an upper room in Molesworth Street in 1898. She received the Freedom of the Town in 1938 and opened The Gracie Fields Theatre in 1978.

Grace Stansfield—for such was her name—inherited from her mother her fine singing voice. When she was seven, Lily Turner, who had sung on the Music Hall stage, gave her the only singing lesson she was to receive. Her first income from singing was half a guinea when she tied for first place in a contest held at the local Hippodrome. Disenchanted by her early experience of show business. in juvenile troupes, Gracie took up work as a cotton winder in a Rochdale mill, a career which though short-lived left her with vivid memories of Milltown life.

In her autobiography, she recalled getting out of bed at 5 a.m. when Old Amy, the knocker-up woman, rapped on the bedroom windows with her pole. As Amy trudged down the street, the candles and oil lamps lit behind her in each window. And in each house a kettle would go on the fire for the tea. The first workers to arrive at the mills were those who tended the furnace fires. "When the mill wanted the rest of us, half an hour later, it whistled. The buzzar, we called it. 'Quick, Grace, t'buzzer's gone.' Five minutes afterwards the big gates were shut and if you were not inside you lost a day's work."

She could not recall doing much cotton-winding, being always sleepy when she got to the mill at six, and by the time she was fully alert, the other girls would be asking her to give them a song while they minded her frames. "Into the din and clatter of the machinery I'd bellow out every song I knew while the others would keep a look-out for the boss and give me the signal to pretend I was working as soon as he appeared." She went to school in the afternoons, observing in later life: "I never learned much."

She was summoned to the Rochdale Hippodrome when a

performer was taken ill and was announced as Young Grace Stansfield, Rochdale's Own Girl Vocalist. She was thirteen years of age but paid 35s a week. The manager, wanting a shorter name, suggested she was called Gracie Fields.

In the early years of her stage career, she augmented her magnificent singing voice with an element of comedy, which went down well with northern audiences. After yet more disappointments, she soared to stardom in a show called *Mr Tower of London,* which brought her to London and a starring role in a succession of successful shows leading in 1928 to a part in the Royal Variety Show, the first of ten such appearances.

In the 1930s, Gracie appeared in eleven films, the most famous being *Sally in Our Alley,* which was screened in 1931. Her stage work was imbued with romance but her private life was far from happy, her first (loveless) marriage failing. A love-affair with a handsome Irish painter on the Isle of Capri foundered. Capri was to become her home and the setting for her second marriage, to an Italian film director. Lancashire folk who went to Capri on holiday found her interest in her native area still keen. Her tombstone is inscribed Our Gracie.

Chips with Everything

Fish and chips provided the Lancashire family with a cooked meal which did not cost a lot and which could be in small or large portions, according to circumstances. The first 'chip shop' in the North of Egland was opened at Mossley in 1863, by John Lees, who had a wife and six children to maintain. He knew of such a shop which had been opened in London two years before but cheerfully announced that his was The Oldest Chip Potato Establishment in the World. The dripping was heated in a clothes boiler.When a 'range' was installed it was heated with cottonseed oil.

All John Lees's children went into the fish and chip business, reminding me of a story told of a Lancashireman who settled in London, opened a 'chip shop' and throve so well a friend migrated South and asked the now wealthy man for the loan of money so that he might start up such a business. "Sorry, lad," was the response. "When I came down here, I reached an agreement with the Bank of England that I wouldn't lend money and they wouldn't sell fish and chips."

An old music hall song summed up the public regard for a delectable dish:

Chips and Fish, Chips and Fish,
Ee by gum, it's a champion dish,
Oh what a smell when you fry 'em,
Just buy a pennorth and try 'em,
Put some salt and vinegar on,
As much as ever you wish,
You can do-do-do without a supper,
When you get a bob's-worth of Chips and Fish.

A fishcake, which was two slices of potato with a layer of fish between, was much cheaper and not only 'filling' but tasty. While waiting for fish or fish cake to be cooked, the customer watched as big chunks of yellowish dripping, newly placed in the pan, drifted slowly about like mini-icebergs. Now the fish and chips are cooked in oil.

When a Milltown lad received only a 'Sat'day penny', the prospect of earning an extra haw'penny running an errand was appealing. The runner-of-errands might persuade the shop-owner that the custom warranted a scoop full of 'scraps' in a paper bag—for nowt! Eating scraps, those tasty bits of deep-fried fat, which cluttered up the fish pan and were usually given to the poultry, was a Milltown pleasure. It produced a crunching sound similar to that when eating *Force* which, with Sunny Jim on the packet, was the most popular breakfast cereal of the time.

The popularity of fish and chips meant there was always a long queue at the stop. With only two pans on his gleaming range, the proprietor did his best to maintain production. A quarter of a bucketful of chipped potatoes hissed as they hit the fat in one pan. Fish sizzled as they were deftly sunk in batter and, in a single graceful movement, transferred by slight of hand to the other pan.

When the queue had slowly been whittled down so that a particular customer was next-but-one to be served, he prayed that the person who stood in front would not be the head of a large family, requiring "fish and chips, ten times." The owner of the chip shop set the customers giggling as he gave his stock reply: "I heard you t'first time." The proprietor turned his back to attend to the order, giving a lad a chance to have a surreptitious swig from the vinegar bottle.

For a lad running errands, the tedium of queuing ended when his order was met. A small piece of greaseproof paper was slipped on to a much larger sheet of brown paper. A cascade of golden chips spilled over it, followed by the fish, in its crisp batter. All was wrapped, and better wrapped, in newspaper, the world's finest packing material. If the customer required condiments, there would be a blizzard of salt and a tropical downpour of vinegar. Then the lad was away, joyfully passing the huddled mass in the queue, hurtling into the yellow vapour which, in the old Lancashire Milltown, was classified as sunshine.

Fish and chips tasted best when eaten outdoors, though on a winter evening any surplus fat trickled through the wrapping paper and congealed between the fingers. Then, following local tradition, the paper would be lobbed into the canal. The dominant smell for couples walking there on Sunday afternoon was—vinegar!

Spring

WE KNEW it was Spring when my gran and mam grabbed us and rammed spoonfuls of brimstone and treacle down our throats. As we stood there, spluttering and gagging, the distemper bucket would come out and the house would get a good going over, windows open, dust blown out and cobwebs banished.

Distemper! I don't know if they make it nowadays. It was a weak sort of wash of colour and a substitute for the lime wash that people had used before for 'bug blinding'—as we kids called it.

Spring brought the first flowers too, dandelions growing in the cracks between flags and walls and, on the railway embankment, the first blossom on the hawthorn. The longer days meant that we had longer to play out after school and that bikes and roller skates were cleaned and oiled for the fun.

Then it was Lent and we had to give up something. I always chose sweets and that was harder even than doing sums and joined up writing. That was really hard!

But round the corner were the Easter Eggs and the painted eggs we rolled down the hill in the park, and the Whit walks when the Catholics walked on Friday and the Protestants walked on Monday and the brass bands played and we stood on the pavements and shook our shakers and cheered and cheered. Especially when the Italians came carrying their great statue of the Virgin Mary covered in flowers. There they were in their red boots and black trousers sweating and smiling, the great statue nodding wisely above them.

Mike Harding

Steam Up!

IF A FRISKY wind swept down from the moors, playing a tuba solo on th'mill chimla' (as they called it), the acrid smoke would be blown downwards, between acres of terraced housing, finding your nose and taking pleasure in tickling it. Walk through a Milltown at night and you might hear the hacking coughs of textile folk clearing soot and mill-fluff from their chests.

Even before daylight seeped into the Milltowns, you were aware of the power of steam. A Lancashire mill rarely slept. Its massive presence could be detected at night as the steam engine and its attendant Lancashire boiler snored in repose. As the engine began its work, workers heard a reluctant growl from the gearing. The growl increased in volume and became a low roar. Only in Wakes Week was the engine shed quiet enough to hear a mouse scutter across the floor.

The spinning mills needed the largest engines, which were of the vertical type, each with a huge flywheel from which driving ropes extended to shafts on each floor. The swish of ropes up the wallside created a gale inside the mill. The size of some engine houses was awesome. At Ellenroad Mill, near Rochdale, the engine (still in existence) generated 3000hp and, in the old days, was coupled to five big Lancashire boilers. The smoke ascended a chimney over 200 ft high.

The town had many mills. An average steam engine consumed between 30 and 40 tons of coal a week. There was soot everywhere and the only beneficiaries were roses which in the sooty atmosphere were not afflicted by the fungal disease called 'black spot'. Steam engines produced ash in such vast quantites that when it had been dumped it gave the impression to strangers that there had been recent volcanic activity.

In the old days, it was hard to visualise anything bigger than a Lancashire boiler, the length of which might be in excess of a hundred feet, the diameter nine feet and capacity around 30,000 gallons. Yet when a new boiler, drawn by a traction engine, arrived at a Lancashire mill it vanished during the mid-day break. Then the sound of the traction engine was heard and it returned with the Lancashire boiler still attached. A bystander asked the driver where he had been. He replied: "Me and my mate fancied some fish and chips—and we didn't want to walk to t'shop."

The engineer was respected by all. He ensured that the mill continued to operate. Even the boss would not enter his little domain without permission, which was given gruffly. Everything in the engine shed was immaculate. The engineer supervised two fire-beaters (boilermen or stokers). A fire-beater was right-handed and, because he tended to hold up his arm to shield his face from the fire as he raked away 'clinker', hairs on the back of his left hand were frizzled off by close proximity to the fire.

The job of feeding the monstrous Lancashire boilers was demanding and the pay was pitifully low. A man who applied for such work to a thrifty mill-owner was offered "twenty five bob a week" The applicant asked, sarcastically, if he was expected to bring his own coil [coal].

Knocker-ups

Old Amy, the 'knocker-up woman' of Rochdale, who was recalled by Gracie Fields, received tuppence a week from each family on her list. Gracie recalled: "It was no use shouting: 'Righto! Amy', when she tap-tapped in the darkness. She just kept rapping till she saw your face at the window; then she knew you were out of bed and went on to her next customer."

The knocker-up in a Lancashire Milltown inhabited a twilight world of hissing gas lamps and sqwaking cats. In the days before special heating, the bedroom window of a worker's house, in the depth of winter, had frost patterns.

He might lie in bed and watch his exhaled breath rising in the chilly air. Paper blinds, on a roll, were fashionable at the turn of the century.

A bedroom was—just that! There was little else but the bed, warmed to blood heat by the sleeper or having the chill taken off it a little before bedtime when a brass warming-pan, containing some glowing coals from the fire, was slipped between the sheets. ''If your Mam was on six looms, you might have oilcloth on the floor.'' Otherwise, your feet encountered plain boards.

Most knocker-ups were elderly men. One of them, who took special pride in the work, attached a bunch of wires to the end of his rod and applied the wires to the window pane with the finesse of a percussionist in Mr Halle's orchestra. A Burnley knocker-up whose pole was capped by a bunch of umbrella wires, bounced them up and down, creating a tattoo on the window. He twirled them with an urgent noise which would have awakened the dead had the street been next to the cemetery.

Alice Foley, of Bolton, recalled that on inclement days the knocker-up gave warning to his customers—'bad morning', 'cold', 'foggy', or 'slippy'. Sleepy voices called back 'aa reet'. For this cheerful, punctual service, he received fourpence a week from each household. John Ackworth, in his book *Clog Shop Chronicles,* tells us about Jethro, a Lancashireman who, though employed and paid by the hands at the mill, thought of himself as representing the interests of the mill-owner. If a loom was 'untented' when the engine started, he took it to heart. The non-appearance of the operative was a reflection on his professional ability.

Clogs and Shawls

The wearing of clogs went rapidly out of use after the 1939-45 war but up to the early 1930s, the textile army of Lancashire marched in clogs. This was tap-dancing with a purpose—an early morning barrage of sound which began with a few isolated 'clanks', rose to a thunderous roar and then tailed off as the laggard workers ran along the street, hoping they would not be fined a penny each for their indolence.

The resonance of clog against pavement was terrifying to the stranger, one of whom likened it to a barrage of artillery in the 'softening up' phase of a battle. Another called it 'the iron-shod reveille' and it made a special impression on a South Country visitor. As he lay in bed, listening to the sound, he thought the textile workers of Lancashire must be rich indeed to be able to go to work on horseback. A Foulridge weaver who was busy in the mill before the 1914-18 war was to recall that she left her bed at 5-30 a.m. to begin work at 6 a.m. As she made cups of tea for the rest of her family, "you could hear clogs clanking away all over th'village."

A clog-wearing Burnley weaver who worked from the age of nine until she was sixty-six years old was late for work only once. The overlooker stood on the doorstep and told her: "St John's clock is striking six, go home!" Clogs were not worn in the spinning mill, for the caulkers (irons) would have knocked up wood on the floor.

The heyday of clogs was the Edwardian period. A pair of clogs was fashioned from alder wood. Those worn by an adult were black, a man's clogs fastening with a clasp and a women's clogs bearing a strip across the instep. A child's clog fastened with a button. The thunder of clogs was heard at school as the scholars walked from playground into classroom in tight formation, fearing even to be out of step. Long-suffering parents had to cover the cost of clogs damaged needlessly, such as when their offspring struck their clogs against stone flags to raise sparks. Even worse was the tendency of young lads to kick any tin cans they encountered, shattering the clog's toepiece.

Sam Hanna, who made pioneer films in colour of Lancashire craftsmen at work, included a clogger, of course. He was fond of talking about clogs, which he theorised were introduced to Lancashire by weathers from Flanders sometime in the sixteenth century. The immigrants brought with them all-wooden sabots which, in time, were adapted to the damp Pennine environment and to the hard floors of the weaving sheds.

The clog acquired a leather top but retained the wooden sole, the life of which was prolonged when 'irons' were tacked to them. The clog-wearer was thus raised fractionally above the ground and so avoided being witchered (wetshod). The clogger's shop, being warm and in use for long periods, was a favourite gathering place for old men who'd nowt better to do than gossip.

The shawl, an integral part of the Milltown image, was made of wool, being generally dark in tone. Some weavers, having bought a plain shawl, decorated it with a fringe. The Lancashire shawl, which may have evolved from the smaller shawl used in conjunction with a poke bonnet, became big enough to cover the head and was frequently kept in place at the chin by a large safety pin.

One lass who left school was proud to have a new shawl. "Mother gave a shilling a week to the shopkeeper until it was paid for, and a very good shawl it was, too—grey with a check in it. I got married at twenty and by this time the millgirls had started getting 'dressed up', as we called it. They had an older coat and shoes. I still went in my clogs and shawl."

Get Weaving

Everything about a Lancashire loom was made of iron. It was cold to the touch. The mill-owner did not believe in maintaining a high temperature in a weaving shed. This process would cost a lot of money and, in any case, the yarn was best when cool and damp. In the bad old days, 'steaming' a shed to keep the humidity high for weaving created an atmosphere which was unhealthy for the workers. What matter if the weaver's hands were so cold, she could hardly tie knots? Or that on a rainy day, there was nowhere for a worker to dry off and she must stay wet till hometime?

For the weaver, the tools of the trade, contained in a pouch on a leathern belt, were reed hook, comb and scissors. She did far more than weave, collecting weft from the store, carrying pieces to the warehouse, sweeping and cleaning the machinery when the day's work was done. Floats (faults) were a weaver's responsibility and if she was 'fetched up' to the warehouse it was because a float had been found by the vigilant cut-looker. The weaver had to leave her other looms operating. She hoped no more floats would occur in her absence. The week's pay was based on what was produced.

A weaver's health degenerated with the passing years from inhaling an irritant dust from the sizes used for wars. The sizing process involved zinc chloride. Fluff from 'kissing the shuttle' (sucking the thread through a hole) also infected the lungs. A shuttle which left the loom was travelling so quickly it could inflict serious injury on any weaver standing in its path.

The tackler, or overlooker, now referred to in the industry as a 'textile technician' would 'tackle owt', though he was supposed to be 'not all there' and was the butt of many a joke.

Wod he's lackin' i' knowledge, he hes i' conceit,
He's a mighty big mon, in his way;
An' if suppin' flat pints meks a qualified mon,
He's fit for a tackler today.

A Burnley man recalls that before the 1914-18 war, all the tacklers wore white fustian trousers. They were not allowed to smoke in the mill and so they chewed tobacco. A tackler had his own little room, or bench, or he would sit in the tape room. A weaver who had trouble with a loom sought him out. It was up to him to adjust or repair it.

A classic tackler tale was of a new man who went round a mill to check on any defective gas mantles. He returned to the manager saying that the figure was 598. He had tested each of them—and they were all soft! A Bolton tackler, having just bought a new house, told the coal merchant he no longer wanted any coal because "there's hot and cowd watter i' every slopstone."

A man who became a tackler in a spinning mill had been selected because he was a good engineer. He actually improved the performance of machines as they were delivered from the manufacturers by tuning them to the mill's special requirements. In the weaving shed, a tackler once maintained a specific number of looms and his wage was assessed on every £1 earned by the weavers. He therefore ensured that all the looms under his control—and there might be 160 of them—were running well.

It was not his fault that he administered the unpopular slate system, by which details of each weaver's weekly earnings were displayed for all to see.

Above: A Lancashire weaving shed. In the old days, when a taper was used to ignite the gas lighting, it was vital to clean the machinery or the 'dawn' would ignite and spread along a line of looms.

Below: A mill blaze. Cotton fluff was oily, being at times almost explosive. Many a fire was caused by employees smoking unofficially. The wooden floors of spinning mills were impregnated with oil.

Above: A trafficless street in Victorian days. *Below:* Those with a few coppers could have a hot, savoury meal at one of many dining rooms.

A typical market hall, where shoppers were cossetted from the weather. Many famous firms had their humble beginnings in such a setting.

A weaving shed held an awesome number of Lancashire looms, which were operated by steam-power transmitted by flapping leather belts. No direct sunlight entered the shed, which was illuminated by means of 'north lights'. Humidity was once maintained by 'steaming'.

One of the great sights of a Milltown prior to Christmas was a display at the poulterer's of birds which, hopefully, would be purchased for the festive board. It was goose, not turkey, which featured at Christmas. The wings of a goose were kept for spring-cleaning time.

Above: A mill was a considerable employer of labour. In a spinning mill, the workforce was roughly in balance between men and women. The majority of weavers were women. *Below:* A spinner on holiday at Blackpool sent this card to the friends left at home.

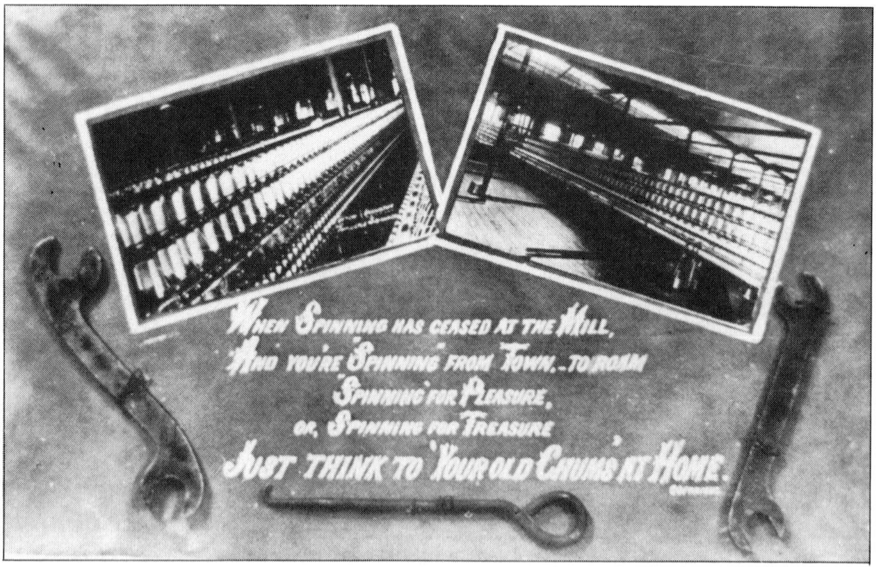

Above: Cloth-lookers needed a quick and accurate eye. Any faults were immediately taken up with the weaver, who would be fined.
Below: The family spirit was evident in many of the Lancashire weaving sheds.

Above:
A skit on Lancashire poverty.

Right:
Helen Bradley, Milltown artist, sitting beside a painting of Blackpool in Oldham wakes week.

Photographs courtesy of Lancashire County Library.

The Milk Round

Milk at thruppence a pint and eggs at thirteen for a bob were produced on local farms. The Milltowners were honest enough, though they did grumble periodically, as during thundery weather when, with no refrigerators handy, milk soon became sour.

During the Wakes Week, when there were few customers, surplus milk was either fed to the pigs or converted into butter, which was sold to the people on their return from holiday. In butter-making, the milk was poured into large earthenware basins, allowed to settle and the cream skimmed off with a saucer, to be stored against the day when churning took place. In summer, the luckless churner was wearied long before the contents of the churn 'broke'. Butter might be wrapped in rhubarb leaves to help keep it firm.

A man with recollections of a farm at Clayton-le-Dale which supplied milk to nearby Blackburn notes that milk was delivered twice every day except on Sunday when there was just a single delivery comprising a proportion of Saturday evening milk with that which was morning-fresh. Milk from the next farm was taken in seventeen gallon 'kits' (tapered, with a broad case, so they did not easily fall over) to Wilpshire railway station for despatch on the 8-5 a.m. 'milk train' to Manchester.

A horse called Dinah moved like a greyhound to catch this train and came back at an easy lope. Every can of milk was full to the brim. On some farms, the topping up process involved water. A servant man who fell out with a shameless farmer used to say of the morning milk-run to the railway station: "There's more watter goes ower t'brigg than under it."

A man with experience of farm work in the early 1930s recalls that when the farmer hurt his hand and had to go into Blackburn Infirmary "there was only me (the boy, aged thirteen) who knew the milk round. The farmer's brother came to drive a bull-nosed Morris, with two thirteen gallon cans on the 'dickie seat', on our milk round, which took in the Infirmary district.''

The milk required by a Milltowner was poured into a jug which stood on the doorstep, a saucer being placed over the jug in the interests of hygene. The milk was tuppence halfpenny at pint in summer and thruppence a pint in winter. Bottling milk began about 1930. ''We had perhaps twenty bottles. They were supposed to be taken back to the farm to be sterilised but were simply held up to the light and, unless very dirty, were used again. We had fun dodging the inspector.''

Life in the Street

Some Milltown streets consisted of two lines of terrace houses, with a corner shop and maybe even a small pub—a format made widely known by the Rover's Return in television's *Coronation Street.* Away from the roads used by through traffic, the street was surfaced, if at all, using stone setts, on which horse-drawn traffic, such as the outfit used by the coalman, could keep its feet. There was a 'back street', sometimes not much more than a ginnel, and otherwise just wide enough to admit the coal man, his horse and four-wheeled lorry.

In Milldom, large families lived in small houses which were set in terraces for economy of space and handiness to th'mill. ''We were like a lot of battery hens are today.'' Some houses were back-to-back; on a grid-iron pattern, with toilets set in a row at one end. Better-class property had through access from the front street to a back yard, at the far end of which was a closet (toilet). A midden was emptied weekly by th'council. There were no front gardens, of course, and the back yards were diminutive, allowing space for a few flowers in pots and a bucket of soil where mint was grown, to be plucked just before Sunday lunch and mixed in vinegar, with a little sugar, to adorn the lamb chops.

The Street had its regular traders. The muffin man announced his presence by ringing a bell. On his head rested a large basket lined with spotless linen. Another clean piece of cloth covered his oatcakes, crumpets and muffins. Another street trade sold clothes props, nothing else. Rag and bone men were common. They paid a few coppers to the children who handed them empty jam jars. On a winter evening, the pie and pea man arrived with his little cart holding brazier-heated food, a sort of mobile barbecue. He announced his presence by ringing a bell.

A corner shop sold anything the impoverished Milltown family might require—except, of course, on Sunday, when all the children could do was stare at the display of toffees in the window. One of the Milltown pranks was to use a magnifying glass and a rare appearance of the sun to melt some of the chocolate in the window.

Every corner shop seemed to be on the point of bankruptcy as customers exploited the good nature of the owner by requesting objects on 'tick'. The shopkeeper was alerted to the arrival of customers by a jangling bell and had to put up with endless cheek from children asking for jelly-round-squares. Groceries were displayed in bulk. Butter, lard and cheese were cut to size on demand. The toffees were counted into a cone made from a single sheet of paper.

Occasionally, it was the shopkeeper who laughed. A Blackburn lady relates that when she was very small she had been shopping and was fascinated by a message on the paper bag—ask your grocer for particulars. "I went to Mother and inquired what 'partiquoolars' were. She said: 'Go back and ask the shopkeeper'. I did but he just had a good chuckle about it."

This shop had a section for meat. "Old Mrs Marsden used to sharpen a large knife on a steel when someone wanted meat—a quarter of this and a quarter of that. We were friendly with the shopkeeper and his family. On Saturday evening, the son called at our house with bones that had been left. Remember—there were no fridges then. Mother made soup. The marrow was mixed with mash for the hens.''

The average corner shop had a deal counter, a drawer for the money, walls lined with shelves which were half full of advertisement boards and the remaining space occupied by assorted bottles of turpentine, jars of pickles, tins of pears, even salmon for those who had had a good week at th'mill. Headache tablets and a very patent medicines were also on view. Of the cigarettes, Woodbines in paper packets of five were most popular. A whiff of Woodbine smoke from an alcove in the street indicated that a youngster had found a 'tab-end', jettisoned by an adult, or had been slyly robbing dad's supply at home.

Do not presume that every working class family had a terrace house. One Milltowner says: ''My dad came to this lodging house where we lived and said: 'I've got a bungalow'. When my dad was cheerful, you'd to look out. You were in for a big anti-climax. We never had much. Always travelled light. We followed him, carrying two carriers with food in and an old leather case. We got off this tram and it was pouring down. By the time we had got to the top of the first hill, the strings had come through the soggy bags and we had to put our hands under them to stop the food dropping out.

''We walked for about a mile through open country and came to this wooden hut—a hen cabin with perches taken out and some oilcloth put down. There was a bed in it and nowhere for me and my brother. There was no water. We had to go back through two fields to a farm for a tap. And when it had rained it was like mud coming out of this tap. There was a goat farm above us. All the effluent went into the beck—and we supped it sometime. I've had that many antebodies, I'll never catch owt!

''One night cattle rubbed themselves against the hut and all the pans were shaking. Dad said we'd put a fence round. We went for a walk so we could look for wood to steal. We went out at night and collected it. Dad allowed space for a gate and put hinges on. I asked him where the gate was. He said: 'We're going for that tonight'."

Walter Greenwood knew the two-up-two-down-roomed type of house well. "From Monday until Saturday the family live in the kitchen, the room at the back. Once a week, on a Sunday, the parlour or front-room fire is lit and the extra comfort of this room enjoyed. Thrift demands this and, if 'Ma' is stern, as she usually is, she will put the parlour's brass or steel fender on the sofa from Monday to Saturday so that nobody can sit on it." He also commented on the custom of open-house, whereby visitors simply opened the front door (which was rarely locked) and announced themselves. "They were promptly invited in, told to sit down and 'make yourself at home', while Mother got up, put the kettle on the fire and observed: 'I was just makin' a cup o' tea'."

In the period in which the novelist wrote, many houses were still illuminated by gas and poverty stalked the towns. A big innovation was a switch on the wall in the living room. When activated, it allowed the pilot to light the mantles on the main jet. Upstairs, a gas bracket was attached to a bedroom wall in the better properties. Poorer families went to bed by candlelight.

A Blackburn man who delivered milk recalls some of the very poor people. "You entered straight into the living room. When a family were 'better off', they had a lobby installed. The wood commonly used for furnishings in a living-room was deal. Sideboard and a dresser. The top surface of the sideboard was covered by a 'runner' and fancy mats, holding a variety of cheap trinkets, reminders of seaside holidays."

The table had a top which was scrubbed to bone-whiteness. At week-ends, this was usually covered with a velvet cloth which had 'bobbles' round the edge. Set against a wall in a typical living kitchen was a sofa which had seen better days (the newest sofa stood in the 'front room'). It was usually a horsehair sofa, the hairs prickling the legs of lads who were still wearing short pants. If the springs were beginning to show, they would be covered with cushions.

The fireplace, a huge iron object, with the flanking oven and set-boiler, demanded a weekly offering of black-lead. The fire was rarely allowed to go out. It was the main provider of hot water, either directly, as in kettle or pan, or indirectly via the boiler. Hot water was transported from the boiler in a 'ladin' can and poured into a basin which stood in the slopstone, precurser of the modern sink.

The 'front room' was for special occasions, sometimes on a Sunday, invariably at Christmas (when visitors were expected) and always if there was a funeral. On the window ledge, or a table just inside the window, stood the cherished aspidistra, in an ornate bowl that stood on a lace 'runner'. The broad leaves of this plant were usually wiped down with cold tea.

Bedrooms of the two up, two down terrace houses were both small and spartan. The average family in those days before family planning took place was quite large. There would be one or two children sleeping in the same room as the parents. Two or three to a bed in the other bedroom. An electrician, recalling his days of apprenticeship, when he removed gas appliances and installed electricity, said it was a nightmare taking up floorboards because each room was full of beds. It was a matter of stacking them.

If your dad was on six looms, you might have some oilcloth on the floor. Most people walked on bare boards. The bedframes were of iron, painted black, and the uprights held little brass knobs. If you had a 'feather bed', then you were better off than most, who had to be content with a flock mattress. When mother decided the mattress must be turned over, to equalise the wear, it was (to quote a Burnley man) "a job to tow thi guts out." Patchwork quilts were made at home, absorbing odds and ends of material from redundant clothing and other worn-out fabric. The old 'uns talked of the days when a poor family slept five to a bed, arranged 'tops to tails', and in some houses they were covered with nothing more than a piece of brown paper that 'crinkled' all night.

The scrubbing brush and scouring or pumice stone was used on external steps. It was fascinating to see a woman cleaning the outside of the bedroom windows. She pushed up the lower frame so that she could sit on the window ledge, with legs dangling inside the bedroom. She would then lower the frame and apply the wash leather vigorously to the glass. The window sills were scrubbed. A rubbing stone was applied to brighten the facade of the house. (It was said of a housepride Milltowner that she polished the tram lines where they passed along the front of her home). "It was spit and polish all the time," recalled an Oswaldtwistle man.

A Colne woman recalls: "We paid half-a-crown a week rent. Before I got a job at the mill, mother had to miss a week to pay for food for us. Then, next week, she'd pay half-a-crown, plus sixpence off."

In the era of privy/middens, which were in outbuildings, summertime was characterised by the vast number of houseflies which buzzed around the houses. Long, sticky 'fly papers' adorned the gas brackets indoors. The early tub type of privy, which was also known as 'closet' or 'petty', was simply a large container, emptied once a week into a wheeled contained by the 'night soil men', who performed their unsavoury job at midnight or in the early hours, when most folk slept.

Jim Cronshaw, a farmer in the Blackburn area had a contract with the Lancashire County Council to empty the tub lavatories. A man who as a boy used to lead his horse recalls that the raw sewage was spread on the fields. One day, as they were collecting the material, a lady came out of a terrace house and asked them if they could get rid of a man's leg. There was momentary alarm. She added: "It's a false one. He's got a new one."

Later came the tippler toilet which, when filled, tipped over, disgorging the contents directly into the sewer. One of the Saturday evening jobs in a Milltown house was tearing up newspaper, or (ideally) last week's copy of *Radio Times,* the sheets being strung together and hung at the back of the toilet door.

With gas lighting, a family lived in half-gloom without realising it. By the early to mid-1930s, many of the terraced houses glowed with electrical light. A man converted Blackburn properties from gas to electricity for an electrical enginer who had a power station. The workman recalls that electric lighting was fitted in four rooms, with a plug in the kitchen for an electric iron. Two hundred units of electricity were available free of charge each year and the electrician provided a free electric iron and free lamps and shade, plus the promise of free maintainance. The charge was 1s.8d a week for ten years. ''We were inundated with requests for the conversion. Each terraced house was converted in a day and a half.''

Brimstone and Treacle

The last thought to cross the mind of a Milltown Mum if someone was ill was—a doctor. He had a habit of charging for his services. The Milltown doctors were clever, but then it was all bottle stuff—summat to break phlegm or summat to make you sweat. Anyone who had appendicitis was kept in bed for ten days on nothing but drinks. ''They had to carry me up and down the stairs for a while.'' Some dreadful pains were not 'growing pains', as the doctor first thought, but rheumatic fever.

A doctor was useful at childbirth, especially when circumstances were not straightforward and the unborn child had to be rotated, was delivered almost dead, and needed artificial respiration and cold water for revival.

It was amazing what Milltown Mums could do in the health front as springtime arrived. You knew just when because cock sparrows coughed the soot from their lungs and began to serenade the opposite sex. Dandelions showed their yellow faces and pretended to be daffodils. Mum looked at her lethargic offspring, following a long hard winter, and prepared to tune up the blood with doses of noxious liquids.

Lethargy set in shortly after Christmas when Mum noticed that the youngers were 'slack set up'. She diagnosed for the umpteenth time that the trouble was—blood. It was 'out of condition'. Some mothers went on about it so much, a bairn was scared to cut him/herself in case that blood was no longer red. The remedies for slack-set-upness were mainly bottled medicines of the 'patent' variety—the sort bought at a corner shop. They would cure most known ills, and also bikes with squeaky wheels.

The very mention of castor oil brought about startling improvements in the health of a child. *Fennings Fever Cure* was only marginally better. It made the teeth feel funny. Best of all was a rich red medicine, quite sweet to the taste, which according to the label was the best cure for coughs and colds. Dosing a child involved some initial brain-washing, quick movements and having a sweet in the hand 'to take the nasty taste away'.

Going to bed and 'having a good sweat' was the best cure for a feverish cold. Every illness had its crisis. You knew instantly when this had passed. For a start, you stopped sweating. Far too many children stopped breathing. Infectious diseases made their annual rounds. It was said that if you had measles, you were unlikely to get that spotty complaint again.

A cheap remedy for bronchitis was to be taken—well wrapped up—to where the roadmen were busy with resurfacing operations. They sprayed tar and covered it with roadstone. The sprayer of tar had what was, to a Milltown lad, a gloriously mucky job. He protected his legs with sacking and worked in a billowing cloud of vapour. Mum stood her ailing child in the vapour and told him or her to breathe deeply. It did the trick. Much more expensive were the coal-tar lamps, something like night-lights, which burnt slowly through the night hours and emitted fumes which were inhaled by a bronchial child.

Every family had an insensitive aunt who, when called upon, did awful jobs like helping to cure a 'gathered' finger, a task now cheerfully (and painlessly) undertaken by one of the Wonder Drugs. ("It maks you wonder what they'll think of next"). Auntie boiled some water, let it cool for a minute or two, spread some boracic powder on it, then held the child's infected finger underwater while the patient squealed with pain. Only marginally less painful was the consequence of refusing to do it.

The bread poultice provided heat for for those swellings called 'gatherings'. Vaseline, applied just before bedtime, was just the stuff for magically curing chapped legs, which were common in the days of short pants. Some luckless children had their chests rubbed with goose-grease, which had the reputation of warding off winter chills.

If you survived the sunless, smoke-filled Milltown winter, during which germs queued up to infect you, it was ten-to-one your blood was out of condition. And Mum knew exactly what to do about it...

Lancashire Looms

A stranger entering a shed full of old-fashioned Lancashire looms was immediately aware of the noise, which reached a level sufficient to induce pain. The operative became used to it and developed selective hearing, such as the ability to hear the threads passing the reed and the shuttle passing the threads within the general roaring sound.

The weavers were proficient at mee-mawing (lip-reading). A good weaver could converse with a friend across a noisy shed without uttering a sound. Mee-mawing worked as fast as you could think. Enter a shed, and you'd hear a sound like *whoo,* as a weaver attracted a friend's attention. The message would quickly spread. The hands of a clock were imitated by the use of fingers.

The technique of the Lancashire, or non-automatic loom, was that established in handloom days. The three main aspects were shuttle flight, shedding (changing the direction of the thread) and the beat-up, repeated two hundred times a minute. The noisy aspect is mainly caused by the picking-stick, which projects a shuttle from one side of the room to another. It simulates the movement of a human arm.

With standard cloth, this heavy machine—a blacksmith's job—was capable of weaving a yard of cloth an hour. It was hard on weavers. Old-timers lost their two front teeth and ingested much dirty fluff through the custom of 'kissing the shuttle'; or sucking the thread into the eye. There were strange rituals. A new-starter in a weaving shed was told by her mother: "Go an' tell tackler the monkey's tail's loose." She did so, expecting to be ridiculed, but he understood what was implied and turned up at the loom to tighten up a part known as the monkey's tail.

Weavers who worried about the dryness of the shed in summer threw water underneath the loom to humidify the warp. Or they'd saturate some thrums (a number of ends) and lay them across the loom so they touched the warp, keeping it moist. Small areas missed in the sizing process earlier would be rubbed with an old tallow candle or even a bar of soap. When a weaver was said to be good at 'dressing a float', she was proficient at what would now be called invisible mending.

Lancashire textiles reached a peak of productivity just before the 1914-18 war. In the last great period of expansion the industrial potential was staggering. Bolton's spinning mills alone absorbed the total yield of cotton from the Nile Valley. Elm Street in Burnley had mills holding 10,000 looms. Nelson possessed 50,000. By 1912, over eighty-five per cent of the cotton being produced in Lancashire was being exported. In that year, over 600,000 workers produced 8,000 million yards of cloth.

There was no standard rate of pay until quite recent times. A weaver was on piece rates, which varied from mill to mill, sometimes within a single mill. A uniform list of rates of pay was introduced in 1892, when the average wage of a weaver in the Burnley-Colne area was between 23s.8d and 24s.

The mill-owners had little sympathy for their workers' plight. As late as the 1920s, a worker who was only fractionally late might have his or her job taken over by one of the sad little group of people—the 'tramp weavers'—gathering at the mill gate. A Colne woman relates: "If you weren't at the mill just before seven, the doors were locked. You were kept out in the cold until 7.30."

When a weaver was legally allowed to be off work from noon on Saturday, the mill gates remained closed until the last moment, prior to which the weaver cleaned and swept the area of her loom. "If a person finished early, he or she had to wait until the clock chimed before going home."

Off to School!

The profitability of a mill depended on having a handy, large and inexpensive labour force, a proportion of which consisted of children who divided the weekday between school and work. The half-timer, known as a tenter, began this punishing routine at the age of 11, until 1900, when the minimum age became 12. Such working for children under 14 was abolished under the Education Act of 1918, although this provision did not come into practice until 1921.

Evening classes were attended by the most intelligent and far-seeing of children. A Burnley man who started out as a half-timer eventually had an education equal to the best at university. Another began work daily as a cabinet maker at 6 a.m. and went to evening classes five nights a week, from 7 p.m. to 9 p.m., and also on Saturday afternoons.

Enterprise did not necessary get its reward. During a breakfast break, a half-timer reflected that the looms were working too slowly, so he borrowed a spanner from the tackler's bench and changed the gearing. When mill work resumed, the looms went at a cracking speed—though the cloth came off them as thin as bandaging. When the half-timer proudly admitted what he had done, he was sacked—more or less. His mother was told the mill was no place for him.

A Burnley man, who left school at 13, began work at 6 a.m, his first task being to light the gas-burners. He then collected the breakfast cans off the men, filling them with hot water for the eight o'clock brew-up. The rest of the day was spent 'carrying and fetching'.

There was a time when the poorest of children, some of whom had rickets, were provided with free dinners. Boys and girls were kept apart, even to the extent of entering school by separate doors. Discipline was strict. The cane was wielded freely and it was not uncommon to see youngsters nursing bruised fingers. Teachers were spoken of as ogres, yet in some schools children voluntarily went early and queued up to read to teacher before classes began.

Schooldays were mainly occupied in absorbing Four R's—Reading 'Riting, 'Rithmatic and Religion. At least one range of buildings which used to be a Church school is now a mosque, complete with dome. Virtually all the children wore clogs. The noise was deafening. A punishment in an East Lancashire school was for the offender, who was wearing clogs, to walk round the outside of the school—on his toecaps.

Parents backed up the teachers, who did not hesitate to resort to their own special forms of punishment. When the geography teacher was riled, he twisted a knuckle against the side of the luckless child's head. The poetry mistress was known to break off reciting works by Byron or Browning to lash out with such force with a cane it was always in tatters.

A lad who in the 1920s won a scholarship to a Church of England grammar school says: ''We had some fine teachers. I am very grateful to them. But I learnt parrot-like.'' Children did at least leave school able to read and write and with a smattering of knowledge about the outside world. The knuckle-treatment of the geography master did ensure a good knowledge of the globe. Wherever his pupils might find themselves on earth, they would be able to find the way home.

Adult education was well supported. Cultural activities were organised by the Co-op and held in Assembly Rooms above Co-op shops. One grateful supporter recalls that in the 1930s, he went to celebrity lantern lectures, at thruppence a time, and listened to celebrities of the calibre of Eric Shipton and Frank Smythe. At Burnley, in about 1932, a slide show was presented by Ponting, who went to the Antarctic with Scott. You can imagine the effect of that on the imagination of a Milltown lad.

Walter Greenwood

Nothing in this world stays put, wrote Walter Greenwood. ''Every spring, Mother Nature proves my point when she clothes the sootiest bush in darkest Salford with a new and brilliant suit of green.'' For the Lancashire novelist and playwright, the most traumatic experience in his life occurred with the Slump of the 1930s. Growing up in a poverty-stricken family, he gave vent to his feelings about life's inequalities with his play *Love on the Dole.*

He was born in Salford in 1902, describing Salford as being divided from the upstart city of Manchester by a dead river named the Irwell. He lived by the Irwell for many years and spent a few of them on th'Council. Walter Greenwood, a restless fellow who enjoyed new experiences so long as they were not unpleasant, moved down south.

He ran a theatre touring company, maintained an office in Manchester. His play *The Cure for Love* had Wilfred Pickles in the lead. For a time Walter farmed in Sussex, but he had to sell up when he was called up into the Forces during the 1939-45 war. Later, he ran a guest house in Polperro in Cornwall.

He vowed that when he could find a suitable farm, probably in the vicinity of Blackburn, he would return to the North permanently. Meanwhile, he lived alone and for the most part liked it, alternating the writing of books with manual labour. When, in 1951, his book on Lancashire was published, he told an inquirer that he preferred meeting people in a pub to being invited to their home. He was shy of feminine company and claimed to be quite without good manners.

His writings have the jaunty restlessness of the man. He wrote of Owdham (Oldham) as a jolly, noisy, carefree, happy-go-lucky workaday town as proud as Punch of itself and its vigorous repertory theatre...The forests of tall chimneys pointed their cannon-like muzzles at the sky which they bombarded day in and day out with a barrage of never-ending filth.

Love on the Dole, his harrowing tale of the Slump years, will have an enduring place on the Lancashire bookshelf.

A better class of housing in the
Pendle country.

Milltown Menu

A traditional Lancashire toast says: ''Meyt when we're hungry;/Drink when we're dry;/Brass when we're short on't,/An' heaven when we die.'' Edwin Waugh, the dialect writer, was partial to ''some nice bacon-collops o' th'hob,/ An' a quart o' ale-posset i' th'oon (oven).'' Most families settled for toast, made with the bread pierced by a special toasting-fork. Toast had a special quality when made on a frosty winter's night, with a coal fire all aglow.

Tuesdays and Fridays were 'fish days' in the Milltowns. Plaice was the choice of those with money to spare. The poorer families had 'garnets' or 'gurnards'—big, ugly fish, notable for having a large and varied assortment of bones. Tinned salmon featured at Sunday teatime if the family had comp'ny, when the salmon was served as John West intended. Otherwise, with just the family concerned, it was mixed with lots of bread crumbs to ''make it go further.''

Bread and butter was a staple diet. At least, the bread was home-baked and the butter rich and nourishing. This was long before the passion for eating slimming foods. It was enough to be alive. Marmalade, marginally cheaper than jam, arrived in a large pot jar. Rice pudding was a general standby throughout the year. Plum duff, served in winter, was known as stick-in-the-ribs.

Lancashire folk liked their savoury dishes. With meat and potato pie, the meat was usually beef. Such pies were on sale at corner shops near the mills, being bought by textile operatives in their lunch break. Lancashire Hot Pot was traditionally of mutton chops, or bones and scraps left over from the Sunday meat dish, covered with thin, sliced potatoes. It was not mash. The sliced potatoes remained flat and distinctive. A few vegetables, such as peas, lentils and sliced carrots might be added. Polony, akin to sausage meat, was sold in a cooked state and in a conspicuously red skin.

Pork products were popular, especially in Bolton, where

the football team was known as 'Trotters'. Pigs' trotters consist of the edible parts of a pig's foot, boiled at the tripe works, leaving a mass of transparent jelly which was eaten with salt. A closely-related food was cow heel.

In Bury it was said: "Keep it dark; it's a black pudding." This delectable fare was made from pig's blood, well stirred until it coagulates and darkens, when 'groats' and pieces of fat were stirred in, along with herbs for flavouring, the whole stuffed into a well-cleaned section of pig intestine. A black pudding, when first made, resembled fat sausages but the shape was spherical when the ends were drawn together and tied. It is still a welcome part of the Lancashire diet.

Tripe had the merit of being a cheap dish which was nourishing and easily digested. A thin form of tripe came from sheep. Black tripe, from a cow's belly, resembled a dish-clart (cloth). When displayed for sale, efforts were made to impart attractiveness by setting it on a white marble slab with other varieties of tripe, the whole display being adorned with tomatoes and lettuce. The udder of a cow was known as elder, which has an excellent flavour. It was sliced thin and, traditionally, eaten with salt, vinegar, pepper, brown bread and butter.

Hot peas were cheaper and therefore marginally more popular than fish and chips. Hot Pea Saloons (known as 'pay 'oils') were available in most towns. A helping of peas cost a halfpenny. A penny meat pie was available, making it 'pie and peas' and if gravy was added, the customer watched the retailer make a hole in the top of the pie with his thumb to admit the gravy.

Summer

WE KNEW it was summer when the Molly Dancers came. Somehow the Pagan rituals of death and sacrifice held to celebrate the re-birth of the world had found their way via the Mummers Plays and the Morris Dancers into the streets of our town. Dressed in rags and banging pots and singing, us lads went from door to door, a few streets behind the girls who had dressed up as the Queen of May and her attendants and were likewise processing.

Molly Dancers kicking up a row
Kicking up a row, kicking up a row
Molly Dancers kicking up a row
My Fair Lady
Cheese and bread the old cow's dead
Roast it in a lantern
A bit for you and a bit for me and a bit for the Molly Dancers.

We used to sing as the sun shone on the cobbles and mams and dads came out to watch and give us pennies or halfpennies which we later spent on Vimto and sherbert dip.

Summer was the time for bike rides and making dens and floating across the mill ponds in tin baths. And summer was the time for the rose bay willowherb to send its seeds floating like cotton lint over the baking streets.

Mike Harding

Wash-day and Bath-neet

CLEANLINESS was most certainly next to godliness to the Milltown housewife. Especially on Monday—wash day. It was sheer hard work. The average woman did not think she had done the work well if she was not on the point of collapse by teatime.

Nearly everyone washed on Monday, as the family knew as they gathered for a mid-day meal of cold meat (from yesterday's joint) and mashed potatoes. On wet Mondays, the humidity reached ninety per cent as washing was arranged on a 'clothes horse', also known as a 'maiden', before the fire. Clothes were 'aired' on a clothes-rack which was suspended from hooks in the ceiling and could be raised and lowered, using rope passing over pulleys.

By the 1930s, many families had the zinc-three-legged type of boiler. "You got up in the morning, fixed on the gas pipe, ignited it and did other jobs while the water was heating." A Blackburn family in which mother was an invalid for most of her time gave her a good start. "We had an old-fashioned wash-boiler in the corner of the kitchen. My father used to get up early to fill this boiler with water and light a fire so that the water was nice and hot by the time we went off to th'mill. Left to herself, Mother managed to put the clothes in t'tub and poss 'em."

The copper-headed 'posser' succeeded a wooden 'dolly-peg', a three-legged device with a vertical shaft and a handle for twirling. Each agitated the water to drive out the dirt. Before hanging them out to dry, she had put some of the items through a bowl of starch and a bowl of dolly-blue to give the clothes ultra-brightness.

A mangle consisted of an iron frame with wooden rollers which squeezed surplus water from the clothes and blood from the fingers of incautious children who trapped them while helping to feed in clothes. The wooden rollers eventually became worn in the middle. A thrifty housewife continued to use it, making use of either end and being careful to keep the clothes off the greasy cogs.

In some homes, the mangling was made to seem easier by the person who turned the handle singing a lively hymn. *Onward Christian Soldiers* was a favourite. When a family got a little better off, a table mangle might be bought. When not in use the mangle, with its rubbery rollers, could be folded away, with a flat top to serve as a table.

''When dry, the clothes must be ironed. They were all folded up, straight, and my eldest sister ironed most of 'em when she came home. We had two flat irons. One was in use, the other in the fire, being heated up. Some people had shields on the irons to keep the clothes clean.''

There was no finer sight on a sunny Monday in the Milltowns than to see acres of spotlessly white clothes, smacking themselves in a March breeze after they had been strung from lines using wooden pegs bought at the door from the nomadic gipsy women. The lines were supported by hundreds of wooden 'props'.

One of the daft tales was of a man who brought home a new prop. It was gently pointed out by his wife that it did not have a notch in the top where the clothes line might rest. He told her to hold the prop in the yard. He collected a saw, leaned out of a bedroom window, reached for the prop and cut out a v-shape of wood.

Friday night was bath-neet for the average Milltown family. Southerners called it barth-night, if they bothered to observe the north-country ritual of dunking the whole family in a one-evening sequence, beginning with th'youngest. It saved light, heat and water.

The 'nobs' had barths when they felt like it, not just to keep clean. Sir George Bullough of Accrington who, you will remember, had a huge works making textile machinery, owned the Scottish island of Rhum, spent a half a dozen fortunes building a castle—it was actually built by Lancashiremen, wearing kilts—and made sure he had th'best bath in the

Hebrides. A highlight of a visit to Sir George's island was to stay in his castle, an Edwardian extravangaza, with animal skins instead of pegged rugs on th'floor.

When anyone got really mucky climbing hills and stalking deer and running the gauntlet of a trillion midges, it was time for a soak. There were really two baths, one set vertically at the end of the other and peppered with holes so that if anyone fancied a shower they could contrive to have water hitting him from several directions. All was encased in mahogany, with a door at one side to conceal the mass of lead pipes. Anyone with a fondness for sailing a toy boat while bathing reached out, turned a knob and—lo—there were waves!

The Milltown bath spent most of the week hanging from a hook in th'yard. On Friday night—Bath Night—an ageless ritual was performed before the living room fire. When God made the world in seven days, he must have taken an hour or two off on the evening of the sixth day to have a bath. After tea, the pegged rug was removed from the hearth and the zinc bath from its hook on the back wall of the house. A roaring fire ensured a copious quantity of water was heated in the side-boiler and that nobody would die of frostbite as they disrobed (another nob's word).

The same routine was taking place in virtually every house in the street, as evidenced by the clatter of zinc baths. No one had devised a system for carrying such large objects indoors quietly. With such a widespread percussion effect, even the sparrows stopped chirping for a while.

Bathtime was a family occasion, though lads who had grown too big and shy of th'zinc bath went to the municipal baths on Friday night. It cost but a few coppers to have the traditional 'wesh all ower'. At home, the small children were bathed and dried off, youngest first. There followed Dad, then Mum. Meanwhile, for several hours, vapour as dense as fog on the Newfoundland Banks rolled through the house. When Mum had her bath, she then had the task of cleaning up.

A child was to remember for life the bliss of bath-neet. After being washed, the bather stepped out to be enveloped in a warm, dry towel. There was an irritating interlude as Mum washed her offspring's hair and set about with a tooth-comb, looking for any nits which might have been picked up at school.

Then, resplendent in new pyjamas, and with a warm drink in the hand, the child would sit by the fire, looking into the fiery void between the coals, enjoying the spectacle of ever-changing shapes and colours. It was luvly.

Ma's Bit o' Brass

Many a Milltown Mum used to be teased about her 'bit o' brass'. During the worst of the Slump in the early 1930s, they came dangerously close to bankruptcy. In one case, a single penny remained in her purse. It represented solvency, self-respect. She vowed that when conditions improved, she would never again be in such a precarious financial state.

A Burnley lad remembers that when he 'came of age' just after the 1939-45 war a family party was arranged and a neighbour who had more than a bit o' brass gave him a five pound note. "I'd heard there was such a thing, of course, but it was the first note of this denomination I had actually owned." Nowadays, £5 is petty cash. In those days, the large, crisp note would have been accepted as a deposit on a new house. He recalls that his benefactress was a widow with a bachelor son who was Something at the Bank.

"She didn't normally flaunt her 'brass', but if she forgot to switch off the light in the front room on a winter evening, I would stand on the pavement and look for ages at the array of furnishings and ornaments. It was like peering into Aladdin's Cave." Aladdin would not have gone anywhere near the average terrace house. One couple, desperate to keep out of debt, started off their married life with furniture made of old orange boxes.

A Milltown child usually received a Saturday penny. It was good to enter a sweet-shop and ponder for ages on the brands of toffee on which to invest the money. Or should the child go for the Grand Slam—a lucky packet, with its generous blend of sweets the shopkeeper could not otherwise get rid of? There was bound to be something sticky among them, which meant that the whole lot fused into a slab far beyond the cubic capacity of a small mouth. It had to be licked or shattered by being brought sharply down on somebody's gate-stoop.

The Saturday Penny became a Ha'penny during the worst of the Slump, when (as one shopkeeper lamented) he had even lost the custom of people who had no intention of paying for the goods. Open a purse and some moths would fly out.

A lad who had bought his first gramophone record—of Mendelssohn's *Hebrides Overture*—did not have a gramophone. Fortunately, his mother knew someone who had something even better, a radiogram. Once a week, at 10 a.m. on Saturday, the lad would solemnly slip the record into place, settle back and forget the staid and sooty Milltown in the composer's evocation of waves breaking against the rocks of Staffa.

More Street Games

The basic elements of Street Games were that they could be harmless and generally costless. In the old days, parents did not permit their children to play out on Sunday, even if they were excused attendance at Sunday School. Some relaxation to this rule was apparent in the mid-1930s.

Whenever possible, boys would be boys, getting into

mischief. If a film about Robin Hood was shown in town, there would be run of petty theft at local allotments, where gardeners found some of their canes missing. They had been recycled as bows and arrows. Garden walls suffered in seige-games prompted by seeing a film about the Foreign Legion, for you had to keep the desert warriors out.

At night, cotton from a reel might be stretched across a street and and the effect noted on bemused pedestrians. Or a window-tapping device was rigged up. It was activated by pulling a piece of string long enough to stretch to the nearest cover. It was daring, for in those days the majority of policemen were 'on the beat' and quick to inflict corporal punishment on young delinquents.

The most popular game with the boys was marbles or 'taws'. There was no 'close season'—just, preferably, a dry spell. For a time, as glass-alleys came into use, these were in keen demand, especially those which were red. The back street of a Milltown terrace became pitted with small earthen depressions used by the kids for their marbles. Success was reflected in the jaunty manner of one boy walking off with a cloth bag holding his treasured collection.

The boys played football or cricket, regardless of season. A boy could play football by himself, kicking the ball ceaselessly against a gable end. As a team game, the main requirement was plenty of space to avoid broken windows. For cricket, the lad who owned the bat and ball was a self-appointed captain. The girls were fond of playing hop-scotch or shuttlecock. In quiet streets, girls stretched their skipping rope across the roadway.

Rolling an iron hoop was generally a lad's game, being both popular and noisy. The hoop was controlled and propelled, as if wheeling it, by a short iron handle. The girls enjoyed 'rounders' or tennis, hitting the ball against a wall. Spinning and whipping a top, hop-scotch and 'tig' were games in which all might take part.

Combined efforts by boys and girls were devoted to

'scrumping', the collection of combustibles for the celebration of Gunpowder Plot. Fireworks were generally pooled. Parents provided parkin or 'moggy', treacle toffee and roast potatoes.

Week-end Pleasures

Cricket and football came first, of course. They used to have their specific seasons—summer and winter—without overlap. In cricket, the well manicured field was, to a Milltown, the equivalent of a village green. Cricket drew thousands to the county matches. "Even the Lancashire League was high-powered stuff that received support from the masses. . . The crowd was good-humoured. People joined in. One man, good at quips, shouted to a bowler: 'Tha's getten t'batsman in two minds. He doesn't knaw whether to clout thee for four or six'."

Nelson's professional, from 1929 into the 1930s, was a West Indian, Leary Constantine, a great cricketer, with perfect manners, who followed that career with an exemplary one in politics back on his home island. Leary swapped the azure sky of the West Indies for the grey, often weeping sky of East Lancashire when he was not able to get suitable employment in his native land. At Nelson, a visiting cricketer who bowled out Leary was told by an angry supporter: "We've come to see Leary bat, not you bowl!"

At one time, Leary Constantine and C L R James, another immigrant from the West Indies, were the only dark men in the region. James, driven through life by a love of cricket and regard for English literature, combined both when invited by Neville Cardus, of *The Manchester Guardian,* to write about cricket for that august newspaper.

The Milltowners devotion to their many famous football teams was indicated by the roar which went up when the home side scored. A resident of Pike Hill, Burnley, has a special memory of Saturday afternoons and the uprush of sound from Turf Moor when another goal was recorded.

Long queues formed outside the cinemas in the evening. The cheapest seats were in what became known as the 'flea pit'. To have a seat in the balcony was evidence of affluence, even though the outlay was small. Courting couples made for the double-seats on the back row. 'Moving pictures' were to have a considerable effect on working class attitudes towards life and art works. They were in being on a regular commercial basis before the 1914-18 war.

Two films recalled at Burnley were *Black Beauty* and *The Fall of Troy,* the latter being the classic story of the wooden horse. It was, in effect, a colour film—colour in the sense that the sequence showing Troy on fire had been printed on film that was tinted red.

The cycle provided a cheap form of transport to selected rural beauty spots, often at considerable distances. Sixty miles a day was chicken-feed to a youngster on two wheels. When the working week took in Saturday morning, Sunday was the big day for cycling. The 1920s were a golden age for cycling because there was little other traffic on the roads.

The Lancashire cyclist used a variety of special terms, such as 'racer', which was any machine with dropped handlebars. "It might have weighed a ton, but it was still a racer!" The term 'honking' related to the cyclist moving through sheer brute force, pedalling so furiously uphill he was not actually sitting in the saddle.

The Cyclists' Touring Club had many adherents. Hundreds converged on villages like Bolton-by-Bowland for special meets. The CTC sign, signifying that meals were available to cyclists, was to be seen on farms and cottages over a wide area. In the early 1930s, a pot of tea cost thruppence. For a shilling, a cyclist could have a sustaining meal.

At Nelson, a cycling club for older people became known as The Autumn Tints. Eventually, the toughest cyclists, who took their machines off the beaten tracks, called themselves the Rough Stuff Fellowship. Cyclists returning to the Milltowns after a trip into the Yorkshire Dales might call at the Post Office at Malham for tea and some of Mrs Brown's anti-bonk cake, which was of the rich fruit variety. 'Bonk' was a debilitating condition which came if a cyclist burned up the existing calories.

Bill Hill and Cyril Cryer were two of a host of Lancashire cyclists who benefited from the coming of the Youth Hostels' Association in 1930 and the possibility of a night's accommodation for a 'bob'. They were fond of photography and later entertained Milltown audiences with slide shows. Bill Hill's ever-cheerful commentaries accompanied colourful slides.

Cyril, a native of Burnley, had a cycling career which extended over sixty years. He reckoned he must have pedalled for 250,000 miles. He was born in Burnley. He began cycling when, having several severe illnesses, a doctor recommended that he spent a year on a farm and took up cycling. Albert Shackleton, of Nelson, was quick to enrol him in the CTC. Cyril was entertaining because of his Lancashireness. Showing a picture of an old lady in the traditional garb of a remote part of Yugoslavia, he said: "She looked nice but I couldn't make moss nor sand of her."

Cyril, a Milltowner who was considered a weakling in his younger days, had an expedition to the Sahara. Staying for a while in a Moroccan town because he was feeling unwell, he had the foresight to chain his bike to the bedstead before lapsing into unconsciousness.

Is ta Courtin'?

Getting to know the opposite sex in a society which was straight-laced about such matters was not easy. A Blackburn man saw a girl he fancied when attending Chapel. Later, he met her on a trip to St Anne's organised by the Chapel for needy children. On the way back, he contrived to get into the same compartment. "Surrounded by all these kids, I slid my hand along the seat and got hold of hers. She didn't take it away."

On the following Sunday, he suggested that they might go for a walk, taking the tram to the terminus at Preston New Road and walking back. "She said that her father was down there. I said I was not frightened of her father. I introduced myself, told him I was in the last year of an apprenticeship, and asked him if he had any objections to me walking out with his youngest daughter. If so, what were they? He pointed to his right boot. I said I hoped he wouldn't have to use that on me. He said: 'Behave yourself'. I looked straight at him and said: 'I'll behave myself'. And I did."

The suitor arranged to meet the young lady at the bottom of her street on the following Saturday. She went to keep the appointment. Her brother had invited him into the house. When the girl returned forlornly, having failed to meet him, she found he was in earnest talk with her father. The subject was poultry—more precisely Rhode Island Reds and Black Leghorns.

"Each Saturday night, her dad made a big meat and potato pie in a washing up tin. We all gathered round the table to eat the pie. On courting night, I had to have her back home at ten o'clock. Many a time, we had to run the last half mile or so to reach home in time. And he'd be waiting on the step!"

During the week, most people were in bed at nine o'clock. There was not a lot to stop up for and an early start next day was the norm. At some houses, Dad locked the door at nine o'clock. If anyone was out, they stayed out. If anyone was walking about after nine o'clock, they were up to no good. Sex was a naughty word. There was no sex education—just smutty talk, at street corners. Pre-marital experience was risky in days before contraception. It was not so much a question of morality as fear of the consequences.

Courting in a Milltown involved what was called The Monkey Walk, which came into use at week-ends, when young men and, separately, young women, sauntered along a prescribed course, each hoping to find someone of the opposite sex they might 'go out' with, ideally with the prospect of marriage. A Monkey Walk at Burnley went along the Prairie towards the Tram Shed. A 'shilling hop' at a local hall was another occasion for fraternisation. Then there was the special railway trip from East Lancashire to the Winter Gardens at Blackpool. It set off at about 5 p.m. and returned before midnight, costing half a crown, a price which included admission into the Tower Ballroom.

Alice Foley, who entered a Bolton mill full-time in 1905, recorded that the monotonous drudgery of machine-tending was occasionally broken by traditional 'footings', when a workmate announced her approaching marriage. This announcement was made in the form of a mock procession down the broad-alley, the bride-to-be draped in a curtain or white sheet, followed by a squealing cluster of well-wishers, the youngest girls giggling to hide their embarrassment and the older women offering ribald jokes. Later, the workers were regaled with "pop, pies and Eccles cakes in a community mood of hearty fellowship."

The average age for a man to be married was 24, with the girl slightly younger, except in the generation which matured in the 1914-18 war, during which a large number of young people were killed, Many women had to marry younger men or remain spinsters. Even in the 1930s, a stigma was attached to any girl who had a child out of wedlock. Lads were lads— and girls, even quite young girls, lived to regret it.

"We had this lad who was sixteen. He got this girl pregnant. She was only fifteen. And at work the other men laughed about it. That wasn't setting the younger men a good example." A Blackburn man says: "If a girl 'had' to be married, as they said, it was looked on as something terrible. And I must say, that it was often a big mistake in itself."

Courtship was devoted to acquiring enough money to start off a home. Anything given for this purpose was said to go into 'the bottom drawer'. After a marriage at Nelson, "t'reception was in t'Sunday School. Her mother and them did t'baking. We had a photographer. And we had a taxi. He charged three pound odd." A lot of marriage 'breakfasts', to use a posh phrase, took place in the bride's home. Honeymoons were a train trip away, Morecambe or Blackpool. Poshness was everything when a wedding was held. You were slightly posher if you went to Llandudno and stayed in a guest house at six bob a day for full board.

Family Matters

It was known for a Milltown couple to be married during the dinner break. The happy couple returned to the looms after that brief interval. They continued to weave until the mill closed at 5-30 p.m. A woman, on her marriage day, would lie in bed wondering what on earth would happen next. The answer was—a lot. Large families were common. The birth was invariably at home, in one of the bedrooms, with a doctor and neighbours in attendance. "My mother used to go to one or two. . ." Mrs Telford, a lovely old lady, brought many children into t'world in our street. Child mortality was high by modern standards.

A Milltowner who was brought up in abject poverty recalled: "We lived for a time in a wooden hut. Mother had a miscarriage behind one of the chairs. My baby brother died. My wife had a baby sister who died. And we lost one. There are so many innovations today—bringing childbirth on, tubes and what have you. Then it was just the survival of the fittest."

If a small boy died from diphtheria, everyone was sorry—but no one was surprised. It was accepted as an Act of God. One family consisted of ten—twice over! The explanation was

A Lancashire Lass.

Fifty-one weeks at the loom and one week by the sea.

that one had died, leaving nine. The wife produced another child, which restored the former size of the family.

Huge families were generally happy families. In due course, if a woman was old and widowed, she could rely on the family for help.

Wakes Week

The Wakes, which originally had a religious connection, became increasingly raucous as villages blossomed into towns and towns extended as conurbations. The Wakes became the annual escape-valve for jaded workers and their families, who escaped to a totally different environment—to the seaside, where waves slapped against golden sand, gulls called and a west wind straight off the sea forced some good fresh air into blackened Milltown lungs. (The funny smell was not ozone but rotting seaweed).

This change of scene became possible for ordinary folk when the Railway Era began in the 1840s. Soon, the county had one of the most densley packed railway systems outside London. Blackpool developed to cater for the holiday needs of Milltowners and Colliery families in the burgeoning towns. Its popularity was such that in the summer of 1919 over a million people from Manchester and adjacent cotton towns were transported by rail to this Lancashire Dreamland.

A unique situation developed whereby instead of there being one general Wakes, what was originally a week's holiday was held by Milltowns in rotation, spreading out the season, to the advantage of Blackpool showmen and landladies. Thomas Mawson, the landscape gardener who laid out the grounds of many a Lake District mansion built with Lancashire brass, was asked to design Stanley Park at Blackpool. While he was doing it, a visitor said: "If it wasn't for Blackpool, there'd be a revolution in Lancashire. . .Men stick it as long as they can in the mill towns and once a year they must either burst or go to Blackpool for a few days. When they are back home, they're ready for another spell of hard work.''

For Wakes Week, the fires in the Lancashire boilers were drawn, the 'chimla's' stopped smoking, hooters fell silent and, for the first time in twelve months, a Milltown was revealed in its splendid setting of heather-capped hills. Impoverished folk had to be content with local excursions, such as climbing to Crown Point at Burnley or plodding up to the summit plateau of Pendle Hill, which was said (wrongly) to be infested with witches. They had cosier quarters to the south of the Hill.

A weaver's family, struggling upbank from Colne, might have nothing more than a bag with some butties and a bottle of water or milk. In especially clear weather, there would be a whoop of pleasure as someone picked out the blue form of Penyghent in Yorkshire. With skies clearing and Bolton, Leigh and Wigan on holiday at the same time, there was the uncommon view from a local highspot of the Welsh hills.

Blackpool, with its tower standing like an exclamation mark on the low shore of Lancashire, was to be described as ''a vast circus with sleeping accommodation.'' The place was quite simply unique. Wakes Week was the time to blow-in (recklessly spend) a year's savings. Flighty young weavers, who had scrimped and saved for months, made their first call at Yates's Wine Lodge, determined to live like duchesses for ten minutes as they sipped their port and lemon in opulent surroundings.

The extravagantly-decorated Tower Ballroom, with its huge organ, was frequented by Milltowners out to enjoy themselves. To the Ballroom, each year from 1931 came finalists in the Cotton Queen competition organised by *The Daily Despatch,* who collected votes from every Lancashire mill. The main object was to promote cotton and thereby help the industry to recover from a spell in the doldrums. Families returned year after year to their favourite lodgings, each little group having the familiar sight of a dining room window in which stood a table, with vase of flowers and the obligatory three bottles—brown sauce, tomato ketchup and vinegar.

At the start of Wakes Week, there would be a mad scramble to get on an excursion train. You had to fight to get one of the horsehair seats and, because the journey was relatively short, a black tank engine provided the motive power. Beyond Preston, the children cheered when someone reported seeing Blackpool Tower.

A CHARABANC.

A Nelson man, taken as a child to Blackpool in the 1930s, was to remember leaving the holiday 'special' at Central Station. "The distance between the Tower and Home, in the mind of a child, was infinity. Home was miles away—somewhere over there. We'd finished with it for a whole week. Mother went to the Blackpool shops every morning to buy whatever food was needed. She gave the food to the landlady, who prepared it for a small charge."

Posh folk went by train to Scarborough, which lay somewhere in the Mysterious East.

Morecambe was another magical place lying at the very rim of the world. "We kids were crushed in the skirmish for seats when the train, hauled by a dirt-stained locomotive breathing black smoke and soot, drew into the station. Our lodgings were known as 'digs'. They were immaculate when we arrived and soon had gritty lino, from the sand we had collected in light shoes, bought specially for the holiday and known for some reason as 'pumps'. Damp towels gave the bedroom the humidity of a tropical rain-forest."

A religious family spent the first evening following Dad round the town as he decided which chapel they would attend on the following morning, which was Sunday. "Can we make some sand castles?" was the youthful cry. "No," said Dad. Chapel came first! And, of course, on Sunday there would be no sandcastle production because, we should remember, it was the Lord's Day. One despairing little girl asked: "Would God mind if instead of making sand-castles, I made some sand-chapels?"

The pre-evening meal assembly in the lounge, waiting impatiently for the gong to be sounded, was the most trying part of the day. One had to be careful not to let down the family by unseemly behaviour or, when speaking, by dropping aitches. A small boy taken to Blackpool was apt to embarrass the family by his forthright questions.

During a meal in the dining room, when the families watched each other and unashamedly eavesdropped, the lad said, in a questioning tone every parent would recognise: "Mum..." He wanted to go to the toilet. Mother smothered the words, directed him to the door, and relaxed until, from several storeys above, came the piercing cry: "Muuu-um!" She had to reply, loudly. "What, luv?" Came the piercing response from her offspring: "I can see Blackpool Tower while I'm sat on t'closet." The family returned wearily home. "The dish-cloth, having been left draped over a tap in the kitchen, was so dry and stiff it kept its shape when lifted up."

Work at the mills resumed. The hills vanished from sight for another year. Apart from Wakes Week, a Milltowner rarely ventured far into the countryside. When someone connected with an East Lancashire chapel offered to organise a trip to the Lake District, with a cruise on Windermere, one of the Flock said: "Who wants to go up there? There's nowt only trees and watter."

Autumn

THE DAYS turned chill as September came—sometimes an Indian summer ran a late flush along the red brick streets but more often there were early frosts and breath began to steam in the air. Pullovers went back on as the schools opened their gates and holidays came to a lamented end. There were groans all round as we discovered that the rumours that a much-hated teacher had left or been knocked down by a bus were found to be just that—rumours. The smell of new leather school satchels and pencil boxes, conkers and bonfires, treacle toffee and parkin.

Dark nights—when we played under the old iron gas lamp playing Raleyvo or Tig or Knock and Run. November with its mischief night and its Halloween when the souls of the dead raced through the night sky above our house while my Irish grandmother told stories of the banshees and the little people.

I would look out at the cat on the dustbin lit by the spillage from the kitchen light and wonder how long it would be before Christmas and the snow and ice. I'd imagine that the flakes I saw falling were not flakes of burnt paper from somebody's bonfire but the first flakes of the winter snows.

Mike Harding

Music Hall

THE LIVE theatres of the Lancashire towns, though frowned on by the staunchest of Nonconformists, helped to make life tolerable for many whose lives lacked colour and variety. Each town had one or two theatres with splendid names—*Palace, Princes, Theatre Royal.*

Some were Music Halls, with a lively orchestra and a lot of slapstick comedy. "I remember a magician who cracked eggs into a pan and brought out a string of ducks. When a big-bosomed soprano came on, people shouted 'gerroff'. It was an exciting evening." At other theatres, plays were staged, "Shakespeare, Charley's Aunt and that sort o' stuff."

At Blackburn, "on a Saturday evening, my mother used to give my brother and me sixpence each and we went to the *Palace* vaudeville, and up in 'the gods' it was thruppence. We had wooden seats and stretched back some wires put there to deter people who were suicidal. At the end, by the time they started playing the National Anthem, my brother and I were half way down the stone steps, heading for the street. Outside was a hot potato cart. We got five potatoes for a penny and a hand in the salt box. In Penny Street, we each had a penny bag o' chips and scraps. Then we went home. It was a good night out."

Gracie Fields, who became one of the stars in the theatre firmament, was fond of recalling when, at Rochdale, her mother 'took in' the washing of theatrical folk. The terrible secret was revealed when young Gracie did not recognise a shirt as belonging to her Dad, who had but two—one for wear and one for wash. Mother admitted she was washing the clothes of those who trod the boards at *th'Hippodrome.* Far from distressing Gracie, the news thrilled her. She and her sister cooed over the gaudy garments.

It was while delivering washing to the *Hippodrome* that Gracie saw her first complete shows. If a new song was introduced, the two lasses would sing it on the way home.

Gracie obliged and was revealed as a remarkable mimic.

A Blackburn lad whose parents had a lodging house patronised by theatricals remembers a night when it was so crowded someone slept in the bath and in the morning a sealion was honking away on the landing.

Demon Drink

In the average terraced street during the 1930s there was no handy pub and what was quaintly known as 'the devil in suspension' was rarely mentioned, much less supped. A shock of horror could be detected if someone was said to 'smell of strong drink'.

The effects of the noxious stuff called beer was evident in the occasional sight of a drunken man reeling and stumbling home by lamplight. If a pub door was open, righteous folk, glancing in, felt they had a foretaste of Hell, which seemed to be populated mainly by old men, passing wearisome days sipping from pint pots as they played dominoes. There had been livelier times, as a Blackburn man relates. "There was a lot of drunkenness. A strong temperance movement was born out of the old gin shops and being teetotal became a fetish wi' 'em."

In another Milltown, a seaman husband returned home several times a year. He had money in his pocket and a throat which was reputedly so dry a pint would nobbut wet one side. When he set out for the pub, he was an affable little fellow. A monster returned, swaying, cursing and hiccuping, amid a fusilage of old jars and bottles being hurled at him by his long-suffering wife, whose arsenal was replenished by her children. They ran up and down the cellar steps with yet more 'empties'.

The Milltown pubs tended to be named after animals and among the first words uttered by toddlers in pushchairs were 'chuck chuck' (Cock and Bottle) and 'moo-cow' (Black

Horse). The story was told of a preacher who was so opposed to spirits of the bottled variety he denounced them from the pulpit and one day gave a demonstration of how dangerous whisky might be.

He had before him two small glasses. One was full of water and the other of whisky. He produced two worms, dropped one in the water (where it continued to wriggle) and the other in the whisky (where it soon stiffened and died). ''Now, friends,'' said the Total Abstainer, ''what does that teach us?'' And an extrovert in the congregation said, loudly: ''If tha's got worms—drink whisky!''

An elderly spinster's campaign against strong drink took the form of recruiting children as young as ten into her Young Abstainers. They grew up equating ale with arsenic. When one of the Abstainers was married, orange juice, not wine, featured at the wedding breakfast. One such was expelled from the bowling club when, wandering into the pavilion, he saw a crate of bottles of beer—and spent fifteen joyful minutes pouring the liquid down the drain.

On the night Old Charlie died, he confessed to a friend who was sitting up with him that ''if I'd my time to do ower agean, I wouldn't drink.'' His friend simply replied: ''It's too late now.'' At least Charlie died without the smell of 'strong drink' on his lips. There was just a chance he might go to heaven.

The Lamplighter

There was not a rush of applicants for the job of lamplighter. But to Milltown kids, he was a man to be envied. The lamplighter, with his long stick, appeared in the gloaming and, lo, light appeared in dark corners.

Like owls, bats and badgers, he was a creature of the twilight and clearly a man to be trusted, for he had a good stock of matches, which to a child would be classified as

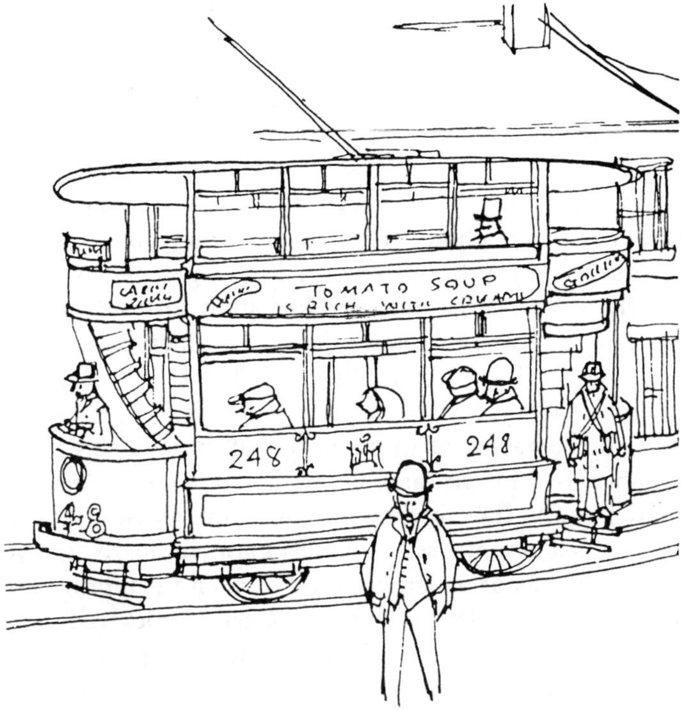

dangerous. In an untypically benevolent moment (or perhaps fearing we would start putting out his lights) he would give us a few matches. We needed them when, in play, we decided to reconquer the Wild West and some of us had the role of Injuns. As everyone should known, when they were not ambushing wagon trains, Injuns sat round fires, smoking the pipe of peace. The more daring Lancashire Injun sucked noisily on the tab-end of a cigarette recovered from the street.

The gas which fed the urban lamposts was produced locally and stored in big, fat gasometers. Nearly everybody in a Milltown seemed to know someone connected with the gasworks. If there was a whiff of scandal, it was sure to have a faint whiff of gas about it. Or so it seemed to a child, idly listening to the chatter of the adults. The man who had just 'run away' (no one ever walked) with the lady down the street was the brother of the gasworks' manager. A lady who was 'up to no good'. whatever that meant, had a cousin who used to have a job at the gasworks.

To stand outside the gasworks was to see science in action. Coal went into the works and coke came out. When the air was slack, a dank smell was detectable. When the council men had been spreading gas tar and stone chippings on the road in summer, a lump of tar became a plaything to a child. He (rarely she) rolled it, shaped it and groaned when inevitably some of the stuff attached itself to newly-washed clothes and Nemesis took the form of an irate parent.

Back to the lamplighter! When he had activated a lamp, children converged on the post to resume interrupted games, like tying someone up to the iron shaft or swinging on the cross-bar used by the lamplighter as a rest for his ladder as he attended to the 'works' or cleaned the glasses. Gaslight gave a touch of romance to a game of taws (or marbles, if you wish). Walk about the streets after dark and you progressed from one pool of light to another. Gaslight flickered a little and did not destroy the shadow patterns nor a sense of mystery, as happens today, when everything is drenched in the orange glare of sodium chloride.

Gaslight gave an indifferent light at local mills. Early on a winter morning, an employee moved along the alleys with a taper, lighting the gas lamps. Sometimes there was a flare-up as naked flame came in contact with an accumulation of fluff. In the terrace house, a gas meter was fastened to the wall in the cellar. It had a slot for coins needed to replenish the supply. A key-like device was turned and there was a clatter as a coin fell into the void beyond. Some families, desperate for money, re-cycled it by forcing open the meter before the man from th'gas company could collect it.

Gas brought to an end the life of anyone who despaired to the point of being suicidal. "Poor man!" someone would say. "He put his head in th'gas oven." Those who gassed themselves were invariably the quiet types. Milltowners who were forever saying they'd 'do themselves in' never matched deeds to words. When an inoffensive little clerk was found with his head in th'gas oven, there was much head-shaking. ''Who'd a' thowt it?'' someone would remark.

After a few minutes for contemplation, Milltown life went on as though the little clerk had never existed. And t'lamp-lighter, as regular as clockwork, continued on his twilit rounds.

Short Back and Sides

The first hairdresser who came into my life was an aunt—a widow with a bull terrier called Pidge. Auntie was the first to cut my hair because she was cheap, giving 100 per cent discount for members of the family. It was a basic cut, almost down to the skin, except for the tuft left on top—a tuft which had a liberal application of a turquoise liquid called Wave Set, which indeed set in minutes. When I left her shop, I could amuse myself by lifting up the tuft of hair as a solid block.

Later I patronised a hairdressing saloon run by another lady hairdresser. A haircut cost thruppence. Some of t'owd men wanted to be shaved. Earlier, they had their own brushes and mugs, which were kept on a shelf in the shop. Shaving was by cut-throat razor. Not only was the process seen; it was heard, as the rasping of steel against a chin as rough as sandpaper. The chin was left white and as smooth as the proverbial 'baby's bottom'. Even more spectacular was the regular process, after a haircut, of lighting a taper and passing it swiftly over the hair 'to seal up the ends'. Mother shared a belief in a popular theory that if a taper was used, I would not catch cold.

A Milltown barber's shop was the place where you could hear all the news that the local newspaper dare not print. T Thompson, the Lancashire dialect writer, made a name for himself for his *Under the Barber's Pole* tales, in which the main characters included Barber, Sally his wife, Thatcher, Jim

Gregson and Young Winterburn. The prose was racy and, in the northern way, the laughs were created by wit rather than tales which, in any case, had all been heard before.

One Christmas, Young Winterburn, hearing talk about food, said: ''Some on yo' fair makes a god o' yo're bellies.'' And Thatcher declared: ''Get summat down thi chimbley while it's free.'' Young Winterburn persisted in exposing the baser aspects of Christmas, saying: ''I call it a pagan festival. Yo' should be down on yo're knees instead o' sittin' up to th'table all th'time.'' And Thatcher replied: ''Ah hope to finish on me back.'' And so on...

Sweating Over a Hot Stove

Times were usually hard but the Milltowners recognised that ''it's thee stomack as 'ods thee back up'' and indulged in a fascinating range of inexpensive foods of a savoury nature and names which seemed strange to—er—strangers. These were black pudding, polony, 'chicklings' and 'faggots', 'savoury ducks', hazlett, brawn, potted meat, cow heel, pig's trotters, tripe, pig's head, hot pies (plus peas, which of course must be 'mushy').

Most of these were bought in town or from a travelling tradesman, but the Milltown housewife prided herself on her baking. It would have been insulting if someone had accused her of using bought-bread. When the fire was 'drawing', dough was arranged before it in greased tins so that it might rise, whereupon it was placed in the oven. The door-catch might be lifted from time to time to let out the steam ''or you'd get soggy bread.'' Bread must have good keeping qualities, so a little fat was added to slow the drying-out process. The longer bread was kneaded, the finer it became.

She made it herself, along with fruit loaves, fruit cakes, teacakes, flat or 'fatty' cakes. Potted meat was home-produced. Suet dumplings and jam roly-poly kept out the winter chills.

"Grannie was a cook in one of the big houses. She must have been a good cook. We all have it in us to cook. At our house, where mother was ailing, father did most of the baking. Any day was baking day with him. He baked bread, made lovely fruit cakes and barm cakes." The last-named, which are still made in the Milltowns, are like teacakes. Traditionally, they were done on the oven bottom and emerged deep brown. "With butter on 'em, they were delicious."

Sunday dinner was distinguished by a roast, usually "a big lump o' beef" which had to be cooked slowly so that it was tender. Yorkshire pudding was made from a mixture prepared a couple of hours before it was needed. When the meat was "just about cooked," and after the browning had been poured off to make some gravy, the roast was placed on a dish in front of the fire. Into the tin went good beef dripping. The tin was placed in the oven until the fat was so hot it had begun to smoke. Just before the Yorkshire pudding mixture was poured into the dish, a drop of cold water from the tap was added, to be beaten in quickly.

The moment of truth had arrived. The dripping-tin was taken out of the oven and the mixture poured straight into it, as quickly as possible. Then it was placed in the hot oven and left for half an hour. The Yorkshire pudding, which rose splendidly, was served by itself as the first course.

The once-proud roast featured at several meals. The Milltowner had a right good 'do' on Sunday dinnertime and what was left was brought out for supper and served in sandwiches. On Monday, the meat was eaten cold, along with pickles or piccalilli, with mashed potatoes and cabbage. On Tuesday—"if we'd owt left"—it might be cut into inch cubes as 'hash'. On Thursday, the remnants would be chopped and minced up for a meat and potato pie or pasty.

Now there's a lot of 'fancy food' about. In the old days, the food might not be elaborate, but there was usually enough of it to "'od thee back up."

Alfred Wainwright

A blue plaque attached to the wall of 331 Audley Range, a redbrick terraced house with a hilly situation about a mile from the centre of Blackburn testifies that this was the birthplace of Alfred Wainwright, Author and Fell Walker (1907-1991). Wainwright was one of several notable people who 'escaped' from the Milltowns and made a new life for themselves in the English Lake District. He grew up hearing the roar of vehicles and whine and clatter of trams on a busy road. In later life, his home was a gracious house in a quiet part of Kendal, with a view of the Lakeland hills.

Wainwright grew up in a typical two-up, two-down dwelling, with a diminutive backyard complete with privvy and midden. It was a 'through' house, not the classic back-to-back which had been easy to build and economical on land. There was no wash-house at No.331. Washing was done in the back kitchen, using a coal-heated boiler, which stood in a corner near the slop-stone (sink).

Alfred's father, Albert, was a nomadic stone mason who rented the house, which faced some brickworks (since demolished). Wainwright's early life at Blackburn was classic Milltown, with knocker-ups, mill girls in clogs and shawls, chip shops, the Poor House—and football elevated by fervour to something akin to religion. In a book *Ex-Fellwanderer,* he was to recall the childhood experience of lying in bed in the early morning when the stillness was broken by the knocker-up on his rounds as he tapped on the bedroom windows along the street with a long stick.

There was a lack of harmony in his home background. He was one of four children. His mother, Emily (nee Woodcock) was one of twelve children born and reared in Penistone, where father had a big ironmonger's shop. The Woodcocks were staunch Congregationalists and she married Albert Wainwright in the Congregational Church at Penistone. Life with Alfred was hard because he worked fitfully and 'drank' copiously. At Blackburn, to earn a few extra coppers, Emily took in washing from more well-to-do neighbours. Her son was often awakened during the night by the sound of the mangle being operated downstairs in the kitchen. It was a common enough occupation in the Milltowns.

One of her nieces told me: "She was quite small, with reddish cheeks and was a saint if ever I knew one." Uncle Albert was "the nicest fellow you could imagine when he was sober." When drunk, he was garrulous, then suddenly he would become thoughtful and ask his daughter Alice to play *Lead, Kindly Light* and he would sing. Although poor, the Wainwrights did have a piano. Mother used to say the home was happier when her husband was out of work; when he had no money and could not get hold of anything to pawn.

The Wainwright children were reared as Chapelgoers. Alfred went to Furthergate Chapel to please his mother. It was at chapel that he met Ruth, who much later became his wife. At first, it was friendship only, based partly on the fact that her home offered a quiet haven—Ruth's parents having died—when he was studying for examinations. Life at the Wainwright residence was constricted and noisy. When eventually Emily Wainwright was left alone (though, one suspects, she was never lonely) she had a remarkable serenity and continued to go to Chapel, which was a source of great strength and comfort to her.

Alfred, tall and red-haired, was a bright lad who, following a grammar school education of two years duration, left at the age of thirteen for a job in local government. In his leisure time, he supported Blackburn Rovers football team and explored Longridge Fell and other highspots not far from the textile town. He used his Town Hall job as a springboard to heaven—heaven in this case being Kendal, gateway to the English Lake District.

Wainwright's glimpse of heaven, which led to his break with his Milltown background, came when he visited Windermere on holiday with his cousin, Eric Beardsall, of

Penistone. Both were quiet men. Both, one suspects, would walk in silence most of the way. He broke his links with Blackburn save that of support for the football club. His job as accountant at the Town Hall provided him with his income. At home, he began to spend several hours each evening in meticulous penmanship, making detailed drawings of the northern fells he explored and had grown to love. His object in creating little hand-drawn books was to provide pleasure in his old age as he turned the pages and recalled favourite outings.

His favourite food—fish and chips—reflected his Milltown upbringing. He was an avid pipe-smoker, creating almost as much smoke as a Blackburn factory chimney. He broke his evening routine several times a week when *Coronation Street* was being transmitted, reminding him of his Lancashire upbringing. When he contacted a printer, who agreed to publish the first of his hand-written guide books to the Lakeland fells, and would not press for payment until some had been sold, he was not to know that over a million such books would be sold, nor that he would become famous as writer and penman.

I have reached the summit of virtually every peak which AW mentioned in his famous fellwalking guides to the Lake District. His books are companionable and his humour pithy—an echo perhaps of his Milltown origins. For example, he wrote that anyone who takes up fell-walking should ensure he or she could tell the difference between a ripe bilberry and a fresh sheep dropping.

A few days after standing before the plaque at his Blackburn birthplace, I surveyed another blue plaque, this one being fixed to a window ledge in the tiny church at Buttermere, with a view through the window of Haystacks, where the ashes (and the spirit) of Alfred Wainwright dwell.

Winter

SNOW! SNOW! You prayed for it, you talked about it all day at school, you longed for it almost as much as Christmas. And when it came? Well there was a street next to ours with a steep brow and we would slide down its Cresta Run on everything from tea trays to real sledges knocked up by dads from old wardrobes and tipped with runners made from flattened tubing that had once been a pram. On and on we would sledge down that brow until the milkman slid and the women came out to throw salt on our ski slope.

At school we made an ice slide in the playground and slid along it in lines of a dozen or more. Until Beaky our teacher slipped on it and broke his wrist. After that, slides were banned.

Then it was Christmas and the Nativity Play when, dressed up in old curtains and tinsel crowns or clutching shepherds crooks we told the greatest story of them all, of the child born in poverty who taught nothing but love and peace.

Then it was presents! And drunken uncles who gave you a ten shilling note! And a pillowcase full of things that were lumpy and magical in the breathless dark of early Christmas morning. The Rupert Book and the rubber dagger, the mouth organ and the orange, the torch and the penknife!

Then to church and, afterwards, home for turkey and gravy and roast potatoes and (uuuugh) sprouts, and everybody smiled and everybody was happy including the dog who wagged his body when you gave him his Christmas bone.

Mike Harding

Evenings at Home

KEEPING the home fires burning was a vital element of Milltown life, especially in winter. The smoke from thousands of fires rose in the thin air to join the pall from the mills. If there was a boistrous wind, smoke 'blew back' into the living room. Or there would be a tremendous fall of soot.

Replenishing the fire was done usually from a common-or-garden bucket kept near the back door and carried across the room when needed. Some coal was tarry, spluttering as it burnt. Other coal, which was brittle, crackled and sent out glowing bits to singe the carpet and be quickly picked up and thrown back.

In the pre-television age, and when radios were crackly, a family made its own entertainment. Those with a piano had musical evenings. Board games were popular. Others resorted to playing cards. One god-fearing woman enjoyed playing Newmarket for coppers on Sunday evenings. Worried that the vicar might call unexpectedly, she and her friends kept the drawers of the table partly open so that at the sound of a footfall outside the front door the cards and coppers might be swept out of sight. The vicar never did call.

A Milltown home was simply furnished. Many of the rugs were of the 'pegged' variety, a re-cycling of old clothes, cut into strips and prodded into position, then deftly knotted, on some coarse material like hessian which was stretched on a frame. It was a winter occupation. The best rug was used only at week-ends. In some houses, it was customary to have a new rug at the hearth on Christmas morning. Rugs displaced by the new were relegated to less favoured positions, such as near the door or on the floor near the slopstone. The oldest rug of all, by now hopelessly worn out, would be scrapped.

A ninety-year-old lady made her rugs from mill 'beatings' and when completed looked like fleeces—fluffy and white as snow. They were durable, too, or so the grandchildren thought. One of them recently took a rug to a washerette and left it in one of the powerful washing machines while she went shopping. On her return, the rug had degenerated into an inch or two of greyish mush, which she removed surreptitiously in her shopping bag and dumped in a litter bin.

The Bread Line

Working class folk were not always working. Years ago, the unemployed did not have the props provided by social security. The hardships of the late 1920s and early 1930s were the worst in living memory. That was the time of the 'dole', issued only after intense scrutiny of a family's means.

A large number of Lancashire folk knew the pangs of hunger, especially if in addition to their economic woes the father drank away much of his wage on his way back home on Friday. A housewife might go to meet her husband and steer him round the many pubs which stood twixt mill and home.

In 1926, when there was a general strike, soup kitchens were organised by well-meaning groups of people for the needy. As one observer said: "It's nobbut t'poor as helps t'poor." Kindly people made broth and soup, filling the basins of the needy. Bread and jam—sometimes with butter—was staple food.

A housewife who returned from the Co-op with four ounces of butter put this in a dish and asked her son to hold it near the fire to soften it. He was less than attentive and the butter slithered into the flames. Mother whacked him, not because she was a vindictive person but because losing that pat of butter was a major disaster. At Colne, a hard-pressed widow who had run out of cash gave her offspring some dry bread and told them to take it round to a relative and ask her to put some marg. on it. "Tell her I'll pay her back when I get my wage."

There was a special regard for children, who needed nourishing food for growth and who, in lean times, showed the dreadful effects of malnutrition. One release from the general misery was through education, through 'getting on', which meant some sort of office job, not associated with textiles. One bright lad who passed his scholarship and had a chance of going to the grammar school was told by his Mother: "Ay, lad, th'heart's willing, but purse isn't."

In the leanest times, long years ago, the 'midnight flit' was a common way out of a dilemma when a family had no money left for the rent. As the rent man hammered on the door, a hand went over a child's face in case he or she cried out while there was someone at the door. The rest of the family remained quiet and still, hoping to be overlooked. Otherwise, neighbours would hear the wheels of a handcart creaking long after dark as yet another family moved.

A girl who had lately left school rose from her bed long before six to clean out the domestic grate before reaching her work as the clock struck six. "My dad had no money during the week, so we all had to be in bed by nine o'clock." The pawnshop was a bridge between a poor family who had run out of cash and Friday, when the wage-earner was paid. A wife would get her husband's suit out of pawn on Friday night, so that he would have something good to wear at the week-end. The suit went back into pawn until the following Friday.

There was a measure of pride among those suffering from 'poverty knock'. A man who had a muffler round his neck during the week wore collar and tie at the week-end. And a Milltown housewife usually contrived that her man had money for a packet of cigarettes, a pint of beer and admission to the local football ground on a Saturday afternoon.

The story is told of a courting couple who were sitting on a seat at the cemetery. Their conversation was overhead by a man who had concealed himself beyond a wall at a higher level. "Let's get married," said the woman, "we've bin courtin' now for fourteen years.'' Her 'young man' replied: ''I've nowt.'' She said: ''I've nowt, but we can put our trust in him above.'' The eavesdropper replied: ''Well—I've nowt.''

Singing th'Messiah

A few weeks afore *th'Messiah* was 'rendered' at a Milltown chapel, the 'tuner' from Laycock and Bannister, or one of the other firms of organ-builders turned up to ensure it would not discredit Handel's work. Just before he vanished into the dusty recesses of an instrument worthy in size and majesty of the Master's greatest oratorio, the tuner asked someone to sit at the organist's seat and, placing one of the index fingers on a key, said: ''Don't loose it.'' The key, that is. The afternoon proceeded tediously, with the unseen tuner shouting 'next' at intervals of a minute or so. The response from the person at the keyboard was to shift the finger to the next key. Meanwhile, the tuner fiddled about with the 'works'.

Almost every Milltown chapel had its big organ and its pre-Christmas *Messiah,* which was always 'rendered', never just given or presented, by a choir which was always 'augmented'. Every local choir was augmented, so a sameness developed. The same faces were to be seen at Ebenezer, Prims, Wesleyans and Trinity. Each choirmaster arranged rehearsals for his own members. And, as ever, the half dozen tenors faced several rows of smirking 'basses' and decided that once again they would have to shout to 'keep our ends up'.

There wasn't much point in having a conductor, for the choir had rendered *th'Messiah* so often everyone had become set in the musical ways. Not even John Barbirolli could have jerked them out of their choral ruts. One year, two lads from the Sunday School were permitted to join the ranks of the sopranos to sing the mighty Handelian work. Not knowing a lot about music didn't help. They were both hopelessly lost in the *Amen Chorus.* The 'amens' came thick and fast. As the patient choirmaster said: ''I don't mind you getting lost. Don't show it!''

On the day itself, the chapel was so full that some people seriously considered taking it in turns to breathe. A special *Messiah* job at a smalltown chapel was for a lad to sprawl over two spaces in a pew so that seconds from time a local doctor and his wife could occupy them. In those days, doctors were addressed in hushed respectful tones. And their every wish was granted. As a chapel steward said: ''Tha niver knaws when thou'll need one.''

Kids liked the lively bits and were inclined to yawn a lot when nothing much seemed to be happening, as in a long-drawn out soprano piece like *I Know That My Redeemer Liveth.* The highlight, for a spirited youngster, was *The Trumpet Shall Sound,* partly because there was some doubt we'd hear it when the trumpeter, year after year, went through an elaborate trumpet-cleaning ritual minutes before he was due to stand up. Would he get his act together in time?

He always did, of course. If anyone was still slumbering when the silver notes sounded, they must have awakened with a start, thinking perhaps they had already arrived at the Pearly Gates. For years, they pointed out the little chap who had sneezed during one of the choral Grand Silences. When the last crashing notes of the *Amen Chorus* died away, and before the Minister gave the Benediction, the chief steward breathlessly clambered up the steps of the pulpit and said: ''Friends, t'collection amounts to £32—an' that's ten pounds more than th'Wesleyans and twelve pounds better than Trinity.'' No one clapped. This was t'chapel, not a music hall.

Occasionally, some other great Handelian work was performed—though not at Christmas, of course. That season was sacred to *th'Messiah.* Arthur Percival, who played in the Halle orchestra, related that when he was leader of the small orchestra mustered for a local performance of the oratorio *Samson,* the conductor, addressing the orchestra at the rehearsal, asked the cellos and basses to 'take it easy' and pointed out there was a difference between ''blowin' thi' nose an' bustin' a blood-vessel.'' One of the mentally wounded musicians said: ''Ower-do it? Nay, ah've nobbut been ticklin' it so far!'' The leading cellist remarked: ''Yer can 'ave it 'ow yer like it: loud or soft, it's all t'same to me.'' Thus (noted Arthur Percival) the dynamics in the string section was settled.

A principal singer, being absent, was said to be 'doing her baking' and would turn up as soon as it was completed.

Workhouse Blues

The Workhouse loomed above the Milltown like a particularly sinister piece of stage scenery. There was a dread of 'ending up' at th'workhouse, though it had improved a good deal since Mr Dickens wrote about it.

Tramps used the facilities overnight, arriving in the casual wards, having left their meagre possession stuffed in cracks and crannies in the big wall at the approach to the gate. A man arriving at, say, Blackburn might have walked during the day from the workhouse at Chorley or Bolton. En route, he had scrounged what he could.

The first job on arrival was to have a bath. While this took place, his clothes were fumigated, even though it happened nightly, at various workhouses. It could be argued that a tramp was the cleanest man in Lancashire. He'd be given a piece of bread and cheese and a large mug of tea. He then went to bed.

On the following morning, he had some light job to do, such as chopping firewood, and a mid-morning snack with bread and marg. He was given a decent dinner, then a jam tea. He was off the following morning, collecting his meagre possessions, heading for the next workhouse, which might be at Preston.

Buried by t'Co-op

As a small boy, I gathered that one should never say die. Somehow it had an unwelcome chill about it. No paid-up member of a Milltown chapel ever died; they were 'takken' or 'went to their reward' or 'crossed Jordan'. And every paid up member of t'Co-op was given a decent burial. For all I know, the relatives collected the 'divvy'.

Chapelfolk were forever talking about the hereafter. One of the special preachers talked about nowt else but the Life to Come—except one night, when he had a bad stomach ache and thought he was going to die. The man who had been yearning for the time when he would 'enter into my reward' groaned and moaned and prayed that he might not have to go—just yet. He'd like to spend more time in this wicked old world.

In the days before the Wonder Pills, nearly everybody in town seemed to ail summat. Walk down a street at night and you'd be capped (surprised) at the noise as lots of people coughed up all the soot and fluff they'd picked up during the day. If someone was 'proper poorly', they'd spread some straw or sawdust outside the house to muffle the sound of passing traffic. The doctors, who acted as though they knew a lot, were just as much in the dark as were their patients. Owt above th'waist was phlegm. Owt below th'waist was likely to be rheumatism—or summat like.

For the average Milltowner, having a worthy funeral was something to be planned years before with a contribution—'appen thruppence a week—to a fund which would provide the means for a good send-off. The Co-op would deal with all non-spiritual aspects of life. They guaranteed there would be a good funeral. So the little woman in a terrace house lived happily in the shadow of death; she would not be buried bi' th'parish and and her relatives suffer embarassment on that last, one-way journey to the cemetery.

On funeral day, the pulse of the town beat slowly. They

didn't go so far as to put mill fires out, but every house in the street had its curtains drawn and people moved about so quietly you fancied that when they left home they'd forgotten to swap their slippers for shoes. One or two of the neighbours had already been round to collect money for a wreath. Then everybody had to go into this house and have a look at the wreath—and also at the dear-departed, lying in state in the front room.

The oldest folk remember when the Co-op provided the ultimate in funerals—one in which the coffin was transported in a hearse drawn by black, plumed horses. Now the 'infernal combustion engine' had to do. The motor-driven hearse arrived in a street where every window had drawn curtains, 'out of respect'. Everyone connected with the dear departed was in crow-black. The coffin was moved (with difficulty) down the steep stairway, to be slid into position and heaped up with flowers.

The hearse travelled at the time-honoured walking pace, with hired cars behind, and its passing brought a respectful response from those on the pavements. Everyone stood to attention. A man removed his hat. After the last rites, there was th'Co-op funeral tea. By gum, but they did you proud. It was a day or two afore your ribs settled back into place. You can't suit everybody. A woman was heard to say afterwards: "Well, I've been where they've buried 'em wi' ham teas an' beef teas but nivver before I have attended one where it were duckling and green peas. I don't know what th'world's coming to."

Of course, the Co-op put up a headstone at the local cemetery. You could take your pick from a catalogue. A lady who lost her husband had engraved upon his stone: "Rest in Peace." Then she began to hear things about him and summoned the mason to carve underneath the words "Till I Come."

Coronation Street

When Granada Television set its new series, *Coronation Street,* in Salford, they chose a nondescript sprawl of urbanity which had already achieved fame/notoriety, for here Walter Greenwood set *Love on the Dole,* and here was 'shot' the film version of Stanley Houghton's *Hobson's Choice.*

Change is evident if you have a chance to see some of the early, black-and-white instalments of life in this famous street. It is recognised by Granada, whose introductory film to each episode shows a Milltown roofscape in fascinating detail. Beyond are the blocky white forms of modern flats. Somewhere out there, too, are the futuristic buildings of Salford University.

Russell Harty, a Blackburn lad who made good as a television presenter, commented: "There must have been life before *Coronation Street.* But it cannot have amounted to much." Almost everyone in the English-speaking world will have become aware, through the television series, of a scriptwriter's impression of everyday life in a Lancashire street, with its pub, the Rover's Return, at one end and a corner shop at the other.

Coronation Street is set in the ficitious Weatherfield, a district dissected by the railway and not more than a thousand miles away from Salford. The appeal of this television series is something more than the social history of a street of redbrick terrace houses. Although no one goes to church, except for weddings and funerals, and "everybody seems to sleep with everybody else," it does portray Life.

Its Lancashire genesis is acknowledged at the start of each instalment as the camera takes in that Milltown roofscape—scores of terraces, roofed with Welsh slates, uncountable numbers of domestic chimneys and, latterly, a mini-forest of television aerials. We come to earth in a patchwork of doors and windows and downspouts. We are in an area of tiny back yards, of middens and closets, of paving stones and stone setts, of a stalking cat and wilting dandelions.

It is all very familiar except that now, many years after the series first appeared, Minnie Caldwell's ginger cat, which would curl up for a sleep in the thin Weatherfield sunlight, has been replaced by a more active cat of varied hues. Take a broader view of Weatherfield, and you see that the railway cuts a swathe through a typical old Lancashire working-class district of terraces laid down on the gridiron pattern.

There may be only one Coronation Street, but in this fictitious town, as in real life, there are dozens of streets like it, with names that would have had a strong local appeal when they first appeared—Disraeli Row and Arkwright Street, Weaver's Row and Maudsley Street, Mafeking Street, Kitchener Street, Trafalgar Street and Crimea Street. Beyond the railway, and beside an offshoot of Albert Road, lies—astonishingly—Nightingale Terrace. Did a nightingale sing hereabouts in the pre-industrial Lancashire, when there were still open fields and woodland? Here, too, is the Red Rec, a diminutive playground, the 'lungs' of Weatherfield.

Coronation Street has changed with the times. Human nature changes little, if at all. There must surely have been, in every generation, a type like Annie Walker, who presided over The Rover's Return for years. She was the typical off-cummed-un who had become a native through long years of residents. She still sniffily looked down on the coarser aspects of life around her. Elsie Tanner was another well-drawn Milltown type. She, in the midst of family calamity—with a son just out of prison and a daughter who has drifted back home after leaving her husband—sniffed her bag of groceries and remarked: "We have to be grateful for small mercies; at least the ham's not off!"

And, of course, there would be the hair-netted, puritanical, sharp-tongued women as personified by Ena Sharples. In the first episode of The Street, she sat in the corner shop, beheld the new owner, Florrie Lindley, and asked: "Where are you going to be buried?" Then there was Frank, the father of Ken, mending a bike in the living room, which was the fashion in those black and white days of the 1960s. Frank's house had a touch of class, in the Van Gogh print hanging above the fireplace. We remember Hilda Ogden, with her hair grips, her treasured 'murial' giving a touch of alpine splendour to one wall, another wall supporting a flight of pot ducks, one of which had slipped, so that its beak was pointing downwards.

What would Annie Walker, beholding *Coronation Street* through genteel eyes from behind the bar of the pub, have thought of the goings-on today. *Coronation Street* does not exist in a vacuum. There have been physical changes and, of course, youth has come to the fore, with contemporary ideas and aspirations. The inventiveness of the scriptwriters continues to amaze us.

The production of the now four-times-a-week chronicle of a Lancashire street is outstanding and, with the Street mirroring life, it will surely in years to come be a standard work of reference with regard of some (though by no means all) of the social changes in northern urban life.

The Milltowns Today

No longer is a Milltown just that, an entity separated from its neighbours by fields and pride. Now much of it is Metroland, lacerated by motorways and with mile upon mile of sodium chloride lighting, glowing orange at night.

All roads lead to Manchester, except for *The Manchester Guardian* which, re-styled as *The Guardian* newspaper, has torn up many of its northern roots. In the old days, when journalism was a calmer and more thoughtful profession, a Chapel preacher was heard to pray: "O, Lord, as thou wouldst have seen in yesterday's *Manchester Guardian.*"

The Halle Orchestra has a new home in a glass-sided building resting on springs. Seen from outside, patrons move about behind acres of glass, looking a little like goldfish in a bowl. The auditorium, with its high-tech organ, has space and the sounds have clarity, even to one sitting on a back seat. Granada-land offers visitors the chance to walk down the famous Street. Manchester Airport, described as a jewel in the crown of the North West, is hoping to build yet another runway in a green and pleasant landscape. Manchester Man (or woman) might travel to London by train in two hours thirty-five minutes.

Rochdale used to be—just that. Now it is the second largest of the ten metropolitan boroughs that make up Greater Manchester. It claims to have the lowest population density. You certainly feel this in the Littleborough area, where there are probably more sheep than people and a border situation is reflected by converging roads and an industrial history concerning both cotton and wool. Much further west, the Heywood Distribution Park has a dazzling space-age gatehouse. At least the mills seemed solid and stable. The gateway looks as though it might suddenly go into orbit.

In the brave new urban Lancashire, a chip is no longer a piece of cooked potato but an integral part of a new technological age which, even in the mills, has revolutionised working practices. Fewer people are needed for increased production. It is no wonder that local accountants smile. The great-grandchildren of the families who grew up with muck but little money now live in a world of housing estates, bungaloid development, shopping malls, leisure centres, immense sports halls, golf driving ranges, reservoirs and lakes used for boating and much else. Generally, the scale is wrong. Anyone walking near the huge structures in a Brave New Townscape is made to feel no larger than an ant.

The old Milltown image has been sanitised and now presented in short 'bites', for as everyone knows the modern child, who has grown up with television, finds it hard to concentrate on a subject for more than a few minutes. Schoolchildren must now visit heritage centres to discover what things were like when Granny was a child. It never occurs to some of them to—ask Granny. They marvel at Granny's stamina when confronted with possers, dolly-tubs, mangles and scrubbing brushes. And on school outings they see everything laid out neatly for them.

A rich urban heritage is reflected in Toad Lane, Rochdale, where a museum commemorates the Co-op Pioneers who began a world-wide movement. Stalwarts, undaunted by the odds against them, are well on with the restoration of the Rochdale Canal, one of those which in Milltown days brought coal to the back doors of the mills. Ere long it will be possible, once again, to cross the Pennines by boat and at Sowerby Bridge, on the eastern side, to join the national canal network.

Well, at least, the Pennine moors are changeless. One Lancashire copywriter notes in a brochure that the moors "roll on for mile after mile" and "have a sombre charm that is all their own." Except that they are no longer just the domain of shepherds, gamekeepers and the odd rambler, but part of the general leisure complex, recommended by tourist information centres as "perfect for both the experienced walker or the Sunday stroller" who, of course, has been provided with themed areas, car parks, litter bins and uniformed rangers. Those who crave for exercise but do not like to have the wind in their faces, and sodden peat underfoot, visit leisure centres or go shopping in the splendid new malls.

Rochdale, which has a grand Town Hall as its centrepiece, rejoices in the 'Our Gracie' exhibition at the Wheatsheaf Shopping Centre, where life in the Rochdale of the 1930s is the theme. Here are the windows from the fish and chip shop where Gracie Fields was born. Visitors see a cloggers' shop and a picture palace. At Ellenroad Mill, near Milnrow is a stunning reminder of our industrial heritage—an engine house holding the largest of the surviving spinning mill steam engines, generating 3,000 horsepower with a flywheel having a diameter of 28ft.

Bolton, a splendid town in the spinning belt and notable in the textile story for Samuel Crompton, inventor of the spinning mule in 1779, is now leaping forward to the twenty-first century and, to quote further from a publication in three languages, has "shaken off the cliche of 'Lancashire mill town'." It remains proud of its history. So does Oldham. In the art gallery are paintings by Helen Bradley, who evoked Milltown life before the 1914-18 war in a series of paintings. Yet Oldham, like other places, is proud of the changes made. The forest of mill chimneys has become a spinney.

In the textile towns of East Lancashire, where the accent was on weaving sheds and chattering looms, chimneys no longer breathe black smoke into a grey sky and in some cases Lancashire looms have been adapted to producing space-age goods. Generally, however, the accent is on new technology. At least, a good number of 'cobbled' streets remain. Local people seem to like them and they *are* durable. Clogs went out years ago. When a friend equipped her family with clogs for a return to the old haunts in a Lancashire town, the population, shoe-clad for decades, look askance at the iron-shod footwear.

The Milltowners, who were mainly of immigrant stock, have in recent times being joined as minority communities by Pakistani, Bangladeshi, Ukrainian, Chinese, Indian and Afro-Caribbean. Oldham's mini-guide states: "Cultural influences include a number of arts groups and excellent Asian restaurants."

Milltowners, both men and women, are by and large sports mad. Burnley Football Club may have had swinging fortunes in recent times, but there is pride that it was one of the founders of the Football League. And the directors are planning a new stadium. The historic conflict between Red Rose and White Rose at ye ancient game of cricket is now enacted ritualistically at Old Trafford, Manchester. The Lancashire

League caters for some of the cricket-crazy Milltowners at a local level.

In the old days, white flannels contrasted with a backdrop of sooted mills. Now the air is clear, floral colour abounds and the sparrows have stopped coughing. Under the slogan "They've Cottoned on. Have You?" the Burnley Economic Development Unit is concerned with urban renewal opportunities and grants, industrial land and premises at attractive prices.

The Milltowns have been transformed. "'Burnley, a tourist resort?' I hear you laugh," states a brochure-writer in a self-deprecating style which goes well among all the modern hype. He (or she) answers the question by stating that though Burnley is probably not on a par with Blackpool when it comes to pleasure rides and miles of golden sands, "we certainly have a lot to pull in the crowds—and entertain them."

Heritagewise, there is Queen Street Mill, with the remnants of the machinery powered by the faithful old steam engine called *Peace*. And there's t'Cut or Leeds and Liverpool canal. The Straight Mile carries it sixty feet above the town and this is assuredly one of the Seven Wonders of British Waterways. The Weavers' Triangle Visitor Centre on Manchester Road occupies the wharfemaster's house and canal toll office. Here you can steep yourself in the flavour of old-time industrialisation.

Burnley proclaims itself as "a town amidst the Pennines" and offers walkers The Burnley Way, of about 37 miles. It is split into sections, each with public transport connections. Here are a thousand acres of parkland and a Superbowl 2000 Leisure Centre. Whew!

At Bury, where the air shivered to the sound of textile machinery, processing cotton brought in from Liverpool, and originally powered by the water of Irwell and its tributaries, there is now Bury Metro, created in 1974, being an amalgam of six towns, with Ramsbottom as the most northerly. (The name is derived from the Old English 'ram', probably a patronymic, and 'botham', a valley). Ramsbottom was the home and workplace of John Kay, who invented the 'flying shuttle'.

The guide book refers to "the rolling Pennine moorland encircling the northern parts" and also to "the unexpected yet delightful scenery of the wooded Irwell Valley." By the river Irwell runs the East Lancashire Railway, offering at weekends and Bank Holidays a sixteen-mile round trip by steam train. At Bury, the M62 east to west motorway connects with the M6 and other motorways, a laceration of the old scenery but a joy to those who wish to attract new firms to "the communications hub of the north-west."

On the day I gathered the information for the last few pages of this book, the *Lancashire Evening Telegraph* had a heartening story about new uses for India Mill at Darwen, a prime symbol of Lancashire's industrial might when cotton was king. The mill has a stupendous brick chimney which is a major landmark in the eastern part of the county.

Like so many other large Lancashire mills, it had degenerated into a half-empty shell but now, according to the newspaper, there is a multi-million pound redevelopment plan to convert the premises into an office, retail and leisure complex. "It is a venture that could create up to 500 jobs on a site where so many were once lost."

The old Milltown image may linger on only in heritage centres, but little of the old is being wasted. Re-cycling on a massive scale means that dressed stone from redundant mills finds its way into new bungalows and a smart house was built of stone representing half a demolished mill chimney. Flagstones from Bolton are being laid to reinforce paths on the North Yorkshire Moors.

The cleansing wind and rain are removing the grime of 150 years of industrial endeavour.

Milltown Memories

NEVER expect owt for nowt. Lancashire folk have fought for what they have achieved. Their fight has been against a chancy climate, against a sooty environment and against conditions of employment which represented blood-for-money. Towns are now fused by modern development, motorways and strings of orange lighting into an urban sprawl.

Many who have become redundant because of changing industrial practices know tedium and hardship, though most people are better off than were their grandparents. The granddaughter of a Millgirl has swapped clogs for fashionable shoes and a shawl for clothes which are stylish and colourful. There is nonetheless a touch of Our Gracie in her speech and outlook.

Milltown life is less companionable than it was. Many families live in skyscrapers. Television is the window on society. Shopping takes place in the glamorous surroundings of mall or supermarket. Grannie is in a nursing home. Families are scattered about the face of the town, if not the country. Young people haunt the clubs and pubs and discos. Holidays begin at Manchester Airport.

The Milltowns are now subjects for the history book. It would be a pity if we were to forget the experiences and efforts of the generations who, over a hundred and fifty years, gave the world its first industrial revolution.